Tabl

<u>*Exposure*</u>

I had a problem with exposure. I tried to argue with God when, in 2007, I was presented with the publication of a nonfiction book based on my life's experiences. I asked myself, "Should I say what really happened? What are people going to say? How are they going to look at me? Should I tell them everything? How will I handle the humiliation?"

Somewhere in the midst of all of those questions, God said, "Hear my instructions and let me be your guide."

I still argued. "God, I cannot do that. You know how mad that could make my family and friends to expose my life with all of its flaws, even the flaws that I never told anyone about." And there was silence, no response. I stood in my room, looking at my ceiling, hitting my hips (My personal way of pouting).

I went on for months without starting. I tried to find other things to preoccupy myself. I even tried to justify the fact that I didn't have a computer. It was 2008 and I still didn't have a computer. Then, the question arose, "Did the men that wrote the Bible have computers? Should this be assigned to someone else?" I shook my head.

I went out and bought paper. We had pencils lying around the house. I needed something until I was able to purchase my own computer.

On June 22, 08, Bishop Joseph Walker III briefly mentioned exposure in his sermon. He stated that, often, one has to be exposed in order for God to bless them. That person can bless others through testimony. Coming from John 2, he explained that Jesus performed a divine metamorphosis by changing water into wine. He explained that a few steps were skipped and that in order for metamorphosis to take place, there must be exposure to the sun. Due to this exposure, change will take place. He also stated that there must first be an environmental change.

My translation to this was that I had to expose myself to others in order for them to skip the steps that I had taken to make a change in their life. I, first, had to expose myself to Christ, the son, in order for him to make drastic changes in my life. I needed a change in my environment in order for me to realize that the exposure was needed.

Now, I am exposing my past with hopes of change in someone's future. I want everyone to understand that the choices we make now can change our lives forever.

My goals are to encourage mothers, fathers, and anyone else with dependents to handle their responsibilities. Parents play an important role in the choices and values carried on by a child. Spend time with your children, teach them to respect and love themselves and others, and tell them that you love them daily.

Pastors, please stop sending the children out of the room when preaching sermons pertaining to being abstinent. Right now, I have a child that is eight years old. When she was five, a little boy in her class made an attempt to explain the word "sex" to her, stating that his father had told him about it. I also have a friend whose sister lost her virginity at age nine. I think that's enough said.

I hope that this will reach many people with outcomes of change. I pray that drug dealers will reconsider obtaining fast money in exchange for someone's life, whether it is their's, the buyer's, the buyer's family, etc. Whether we realize it or not, multiple people are affected by drugs.

The characters in this book are real, just not all of the names. I changed the names because I have no intentions of causing dislike of any kind to some of these characters. I believe that they played an active roll in the lessons of my past.

The events are also real. I chose these specific events because they, too, play an important roll in my present decision-making. Never underestimate life and the changes that may come.

The Aggressive Id

"Are you seeing me and someone else?"

"What?"

"Are you………….."

"Shut up."

"Why can't you answer me?"

I felt Gregory's hand across my face. I didn't say another word. All that I could do was look down at my hands. I held them open, staring as if I needed a response from them. I was amazed, pissed, and hurt at the same time. I couldn't figure out whether or not to hit back or cry. He was much larger than I was. If I hit back, he would return the favor, but harder. If I cry, he would tell me that I'm just a kid. Therefore, I sat there with my head down.

He took me to his place.

"Go in the room and take off your clothes."

I went. I knew I wouldn't be able to satisfy him. I was hurt. I couldn't get turned on. He was right behind me, headed towards his room, taking off his shirt as he was walking. As we entered the room, I turned to him. I took off my pants. He reached down to feel me.

"You're so wet…..Bend over."

I bent over for him to enter me. I moaned, pretending to enjoy every minute of his sex, praying that he would soon be finished, crying because my back was to him.

I met Gregory my freshmen year in High School. I had seen him on numerous occasions in the newspaper, television, and photos that other girls had taken of him. To me, he was just another High School football star. I never thought that he would come into my life the way he did.

My sister and I were headed to the mall when her boyfriend called. He told her to meet him at Burger King. She went in while I stayed in the car. She stated that she would be right back, but 15 minutes had already gone by. Annoyed, I got out of the car. I walked pass Gregory.

"Hey."

"Hey," I said indifferently.

I was so frustrated with my sister, I did not notice Gregory had closed his car door and was following me. He walked to my sister.

"Is this your little sister?"

"Yes."

"She's pretty."

My sister raised her brow. "Now don't be trying to hit on my sister."

"I'm not. I'm just telling you she's cute."

"Aw."

"What are y'all about to do?"

"I'm taking her to the mall. Then, we're going to go to Phillip's house."

"I'm going to come by there."

"Why?"

"Just to hang out with y'all."

He smirked a little. She read right into him.

"She's too young for you!"

He blew her off. "Phillip, call me."

After leaving the mall, we stopped by Phillip's. Gregory was already there. I was nervous.

"I'm scared of him."

"Don't be scared. He's not here to see you. He already has a girlfriend."

We walked into Phillip's apartment. The talking ceased between Phillip and Gregory. Phillip walked to Tina.

"Hey, I just ordered a pizza. Let's go pick it up."

They headed towards the door. I grabbed her.

"Don't leave me here."

I knew she would. I was so afraid. Tina jerked away.

"Tree, we're coming right back."

The door closed. They were gone. I stood at the door, afraid to turn around.

"Are you scared of me?"

I leaned against the door.

"A little."

"Why? I'm not going to hurt you. Come, sit down."

I sat across from him. He came over and sat beside me. I was nervous.

"Why does your family call you Tree?"

"Because my middle name is Patrice."

"You know, you're a really pretty girl."

"Thanks."

He was very close to me. I stood and moved to the loveseat, pretending to watch the television as time passed.

"Why you move?"

"You were so close to me."

"I make you uncomfortable?"

I nodded. He came over and touched the side of my face. He leaned towards me. We kissed. I was extremely nervous. We were startled by the turning of the doorknob. Tina and Phillip were at the door. I let out a sigh of relief.

The next day my sister came to me.

"Did you kiss him?"

Embarrassed, I said, "Yes."

"He told Phillip. Phillip said Gregory wants to see you again."

"He's too old for me. Plus, when I'm in his presence, I get so nervous my underwear gets wet."

Tina laughed, "Fool, you are crazy."

"I'm serious. How old is he?"

"He's about twenty."

"You know that's too old for me. Why would he want me? I'm a kid."

"Yeah but, you're pretty. And you got a big butt. That's what he likes."

4

"Shut-up."

The thought of him made me nervous all over again.

The next weekend, Tina wanted to go back to Phillip's apartment. I went with her because I wanted to see my friend, Shauna. Shauna just happened to be Gregory's little sister. He didn't live with them. Therefore, I knew that I wouldn't have to worry about running into him.

Shauna's mother told me that she wasn't home. We left, heading to Phillip's. As we arrived, I noticed Gregory's car parked beside Phillip's car. I sighed. I turned to Tina.

"Please leave."

"What?"

"I don't want to go in there."

"Why?"

"He makes me feel really funny."

She laughed at the fact that I feared him.

"Why you so scared of him?"

"I don't know. I can't really explain how he makes me feel."

"We won't be here long."

"Don't leave me here with him."

"I won't."

"Promise." I demanded.

"I promise."

We got out of the car and walked into the apartment. Gregory smiled. I felt faint.

"Sup, Tree?"

"Nothing, Phil."

"Greg, you know what's funny about her? When you're here, she won't say anything. When you're not, we can't get her to shut-up."

Gregory smiled as he walked towards me. He embraced my hand slowly.

"Come with me to the back."

"Why?"

"I want to talk to you."

"Why don't we go outside or something?"

"It's too hot. Come on."

He tugged me a little.

"Tree, go with him. He wanted to see you."

"You knew he would be here?"

"Yeah. Just go."

"Tina."

"Just go. He won't hurt you. I'm not leaving."

I went.

We were sitting on the bed in Phillip's room.

"Layla, how old are you?"

"I'm fourteen."

I looked at him to see his reaction. He didn't seem to care.

"You are young. I remember when you brought my order out at Sonics. I thought you were really pretty. I told my girlfriend. She got a little jealous. How were you working there if you're only fourteen?"

"I lied about my age. My mom wasn't making enough to pay my allowance. So, I lied to make the money."

"Why'd you stop?"

"My mom got tired of picking me up late. She came to complain about it and told them how old I really was."

He looked in to my eyes.

"Your lips are soft. I've been wanting to feel them again."

My stomach began to churn. He leaned over to kiss me. I moved away.

"Don't stop me."

He was forceful. I felt weak and vulnerable.

"Kiss me."

We kissed. He lightly put his hand on my back and lifted himself onto me. My legs opened to let him in. He looked at me.

"You're so beautiful."

We kissed again. He unbuttoned my pants. I looked up at him, wanting to say something that would change the mood, making him not want to take this any farther.

"What about your girlfriend?" I whispered.

"What about her?" He pulled my pants down.

6

I didn't respond.

"Lay back."

"I can't............"

"Lay back."

His head was between my legs. I grabbed the sheets. I bit my top lip to stop my moan. My legs and butt tightened. My heart was beating so fast. The sheets became damp from my secretion.

"Please stop."

"Let me finish."

I begged him to stop as tears rolled down my eyes.

"I can't take it anymore."

He stopped. His face was wet. He was hard. He wiped my remnants from his face and kissed me. I was so confused, I wept.

"What do you want from me?"

"I don't know. There's something about you that I really like."

"Why me?"

"I don't know that either."

That's not what I wanted to hear, but it was the truth.

We walked out of the room. I could hear my sister in the bedroom with Phillip. I sat on the couch. He sat by me with his hand on my thigh. We were silent. I was thinking about what had happened.

"Will you come back over here?"

"I don't know."

I couldn't get myself together. *What had he done to me?* I reassured myself that I wouldn't come back. He would not have me that way again.

Two weeks had gone by. He had been calling our house, talking to Tina about bringing me to Phillip's so that he could see me. I tried to avoid him.

"Layla, why haven't you been coming with Tina?"

"I just wanted to forget everything that happened."

"Why?"

"You're too old for me and you make me nervous. Plus, I'm afraid you'll hurt me."

"I won't hurt you. I just want to see you."

"No."

Angrily, he said, "I'm coming over there. I know your mom is gone to work."

"My brother will be here."

"What the hell is he going to do?"

I didn't respond. I knew my brother wouldn't allow anything to happen between Gregory and me.

"Put Tina back on the phone."

He seemed frustrated. I could hear her talking as she walked into my mom's room.

"Yeah, I'll tell him he can use the car to go see his girlfriend."

Ten minutes later, the doorbell rang. My sister had given my brother the keys to the car so that he could go to his girlfriend's house. I ran to my room, knowing he was at the door. My sister went to the front to let Phillip and Gregory in. I sat on the bed. I couldn't think. Gregory walked into the room.

"Hey."

"Hey."

"Come over here. Give me a hug."

He locked the bedroom door and came towards me. I leaned against the wall. He didn't kiss me. He went straight for my pants. I couldn't move. I leaned against the wall as he unbuttoned them. He was on his knees again. He didn't stop. He put my legs around his neck. He threw me onto the bed.

"Stop," was all that I could muster.

"No."

"Please."

I was weak. Tears were rolling again.

"Do you know how bad I've been wanting to see you?"

"You have a girlfriend!"

"Shut-up!"

I couldn't stop him. He pulled himself up to my face. Looked me in the eyes.

"Are you afraid I'm going to hurt you?"

8

I swallowed.

"Yes…yes, I'm so scared."

He rubbed my tears away.

"Stop crying. I really like you."

He kissed me softly, pulled my shirt over my head, and stared. "Damn, you're so beautiful."

He stood to take off his pants and underwear. He was big. I became reluctant.

"I…I can't."

"Come here."

He pulled me to him, softly rubbing my body. I succumbed. He entered me. We both gasped for breath. I clenched the cover as he moved back and forth. He continued until we could take no more.

My cousin had a crush on Gregory for a long time, but for a year, she had been sleeping with my neighbor, Travis. One day, she walked into our house.

"Hey, y'all."

"Hey."

My brother asked her, "What are you doing over here?"

"Getting ready to go next door… Hey, I rode by here last week and saw Gregory's car over here."

"Yeah, he and Phillip came by to see Tina."

Tina heard them chatting as she walked into the room. She mischievously grinned at me, knowing that Gregory was here for me.

"Tree, Gregory is fine, ain't he?" my cousin asked.

"He's okay. Girls are always throwing themselves at him. I don't know why he's such a big deal to them."

"He's fine! That's why."

She seemed annoyed with me. While frowning at me, she said, "I'm gonna go. You don't have any taste."

"Bye."

I thought to myself, *if she only knew.*

Gregory and I had been sneaking around all summer. I assumed things would change when school started back. He was in college. I was in high school. I was sure things would change. I had told my friends, Chase and Leslie, about my summer with Gregory. They were a little amazed. I don't really think they believed me at first. That changed when we had to meet at Leslie's house while her mom was at work.

We had been sleeping around all over the town. At night, when he just had to have me, we would park on a back road, close to a cow pasture. During the day, he would pick me up or I would have someone to take me over there. I knew he didn't love me. I knew it was just sex. We had absolutely nothing in common. We didn't talk about anything other than where and what time we were meeting, or what position he wanted me in.

Unfortunately, I didn't feel the same way. I was in love with him. I knew I couldn't tell him that. Therefore, I did everything possible to satisfy him. Some days, he seemed angry when he met me. It was as if he needed to use me to get out his frustration. It would hurt to know that there was something on his mind and he couldn't talk to me about it. To make up for that, I would try so hard to please him, giving him my best only for him to treat me as if I had let him down. I would cry about it later.

I made my friends promise not to tell anyone. My brother still didn't know. He didn't find out the truth until basketball season. When the season started, Gregory began to come to the games. He would sit on the opponent side.

One day, after one of the games, he told my brother, "Your little sister is cute."
"Touch my sister and I'll kill ya."
He laughed. My brother didn't.
"What would you say about me talking to her?"
"You know she's too young for you."
"How old are you, Tree?" Gregory asked.
"I'm fifteen."

He raised his brow as if something were wrong.

"My birthday was in October."

"Aw."

I walked away. I was a little upset with him for not knowing. I remember telling him that my birthday was coming. He didn't even acknowledge it.

My brother and I went to the gas station after the game. We would always go there to hang out with our friends after the home games. Gregory and Phillip stopped also.

"What up, Black?"

"Nothing, what's up, Phil?"

My brother gave dap to Phil and Gregory as they were getting out of the car. He and Phil walked into the store. Gregory stood outside talking to some of the basketball players. He motioned for me to come over after the conversation.

"You gonna meet me tonight?"

"Yeah. Where?"

"Tell your sister to drop you off at my place on her way to Phillips."

"Okay."

"Tree, get the hell away from him!" my brother yelled as he was walking out of the store.

I walked away. I could hear Gregory laughing. I was embarrassed. He knew my brother would be livid if he knew the truth. I thought to myself, *he'd probably kill both of us.*

The next game was in Huntington. It was a small town about twelve miles from home. I rode with my brother. Gregory was there with Phillip. After the game, we stopped at McDonald's to meet our friends. Our team was on a winning streak. We met up to discuss the game.

Gregory and Phillip pulled into one of the parking spaces.

They began to chat with some of the players. My brother went over to chat also. I stayed by the car. I wanted to keep my distance. One of my adversaries walked over and hugged Gregory. I was upset, but couldn't show it. I decided I would make him aware of my dislike for her the next time we were alone. She had been trying to give me a hard time at school.

On the way home my brother said, "I saw Gregory looking at you at McDonald's."

"Really?" I was excited, but tried to hide it in my voice. At least someone saw that he acknowledged me.

"Yeah, he's been coming to the games too. I've never seen him at one of our games until now. I know he's dating that white girl, Sarah. He better quit looking at you."

"He just does that to upset you."

"No, I think he wants to fuck you."

I was silent. That hurt. *Is that all that he wants from me? Sex?* We sat in silence until we got home.

Gregory and Phillip stopped by the house on their way home. My brother and his girlfriend were in his room. Phillip walked back to our room to see Tina. Gregory came in and sat by me on the couch in the living room.

"What will your brother say when comes in here and sees us sitting together?"

"I don't know."

"I'm going to tell him."

"Are you crazy?"

"He's gonna find out eventually."

"Not by me."

We heard one of the doors open. My brother and his girlfriend were standing in the hallway. His eyes became red. Gregory had his hand on my thigh.

"Where's Tina and Phillip", my brother asked.

"In the back", Gregory replied.

"Tree, you need to go to momma's room."

"No she doesn't. She's gonna sit here with me."

"I told you she's too young."

Kurt's voice was rising. He was angry.

"Kurt, I've been messing with your sister since this summer. Do

12

you really think I've been coming over here to hang out with Tina and Phillip?"

Kurt looked pissed. His girlfriend pulled him into his room. He came back into the living room.

"Man, don't hurt my sister."

"I'm not."

I sighed. *Finally, we don't have to hide from him.*

Kurt's acceptance of our relationship made it easier for me to spend time with Gregory after the games. Gregory began to drive to the games to bring me home afterwards.

People began to gossip. One day, when I walked into the school, one of the girls met me at the entrance of the cafeteria.

"Are you sleeping with Gregory? I hope not, cause he's with Sarah. I saw them in Wal-Mart together last night." She rolled her eyes and walked away. I didn't answer her. My stomach churned. My heart was crushed.

I couldn't eat all day. He didn't call me last night. I knew he was with someone else. I was so hurt. I knew she was telling the truth. *But, why did she have to approach me in front of everyone?* I knew my rivals wanted to see my expression.

After school, I decided to take a long walk on a back road. I needed time to think. I put on my sweats and left. I had walked about two miles from home when I heard a car coming. I stopped, shocked to see him. *How did he know where I was?*

"Why are you walking this back road by yourself?"

"I just needed to get away."

I looked at him, trying to hold back my tears.

"Get in."

"I want to finish walking."

"Get in. I'll help you work out."

I got in the car. I felt a lump in my throat. I thought I would burst into tears at any minute.

"What's wrong with you?"

"Nothing."

The car stopped.

"Why are you crying?"

"One of the girls at school told me that you were with Sarah last night."

He was nonchalant. "So."

"So, why aren't you with her now?"

"Cause I'm with you."

"Am I just sex to you?"

"Do you possibly think you could love me?"

He said that as if to say, "What do you think?"

I gasped for breathe. I wanted to get out.

"Please let me out."

"No, we're going to my place."

"I can't have sex with you now."

"Why?"

"Because I'm hurting."

I could barely breathe.

"You're a kid, Layla. You're too young to love me."

"Do you love her?"

"Does it matter?"

"Why would you continue sleeping with me when you love someone else?"

"We're just having sex! That's it! Sex!"

He took me to his house. I said nothing. I gave him what he wanted.

"Are you ready to go home?"

"Yeah."

"Let's go."

We got into the car. I was quiet. He looked at me.

"You weren't wet."

I said nothing. I sat in a daze, looking out the window.

"Did you hear me?"

"Yes."

"Look at me, damnit!"

He grabbed my face. My tears rolled.

"Why are you always crying? What's wrong with you?"

"I'm hurting. My heart is broken. What do you expect? I do

everything I can to satisfy you, but I'm nothing to you but sex."
I was surprised that I was able to express myself to him. I folded my arms and continued looking out.
"You're too young to love me."
We sat in silence until he pulled into the yard.
"You better wipe your face before you go in there."
I opened the door to get out. He grabbed my arm and pulled me towards him.
"Kiss me."
I kissed him.
"Call me when you get home from school tomorrow."
I walked into the house. My mom was there.
"Where have you been? Why did you just get out of the car with Gregory?"
"I went to Shauna's. He brought me home."
My brother was standing in the doorway, looking as if I'd been caught. As I walked to my room, my mom said," I saw Gregory last night with some white girl."
I walked to my room, shoved my head in my pillow, and cried myself to sleep.

Gregory had killed my self-esteem. He made me feel worthless, as if I were good for nothing, but sex. *How was I too young to love him, but not young enough for him to continuously call me for sex?*

I awakened in the middle of the night. I prayed. I had to pray. God was the only person that could keep me sane. I couldn't talk to my family about the way I felt. They were in their own little world. If I told my brother, he would be angry, but couldn't really do anything about it. My sister would tell Phillip. That wouldn't help. If I told my friends, they would just tell the others at school. Then, I would look like a fool. Therefore, I just talked to God. I told him everything. I talked and cried until I fell asleep again.

I continued sleeping with Gregory. I couldn't kick my addiction. So, I continued being the fool.

One day, he dropped me off while my neighbor was

outside washing his car. He leaned over and kissed me before I got out. My neighbor saw the whole thing. He waited until my mom was home. Then, he came over, called her outside, and told her everything. She came back in the house. She was angry. She called me to the kitchen.

"Some of the people at work told me that they had been seeing Gregory's car over here. I thought it was for either Tina or Kurt. My neighbor just told me that he saw you two together. Have you been messing with him?"

"No ma'am."

"Don't you lie to me!"

"I'm not!"

She walked away. She knew that I had lied to her.

A few weeks later, my mom switched shifts. She left work early one day after getting sick. Tina was gone with Phillip. My brother was in the kitchen cooking. I was in the room with Gregory. Gregory was finishing when my brother yelled, "Momma's here, momma's here."

Gregory ran to the front, while I was in the room putting on my clothes. She walked to her room.

"Layla, come here."

I went to her room.

"Were you having sex with him?"

"No."

There was semen on the bottom of my shirt. I covered it with my hand. I was caught.

"Are you sure?"

"Yes."

She walked outside to talk to Gregory. I was so embarrassed. I couldn't hear them. I waited until she walked back into the house. Then, I went outside.

"What did she say?"

"She called me a freak. She told me that you were too young for me."

"What else did she say?"

16

He was just as shocked as I was. He just pulled me to him, kissed me, and left.

I walked back in the house. My brother was standing in the kitchen in shock. My mom was in her room with the door closed. I went to my room and locked the door. I thought she would beat me until I was unconscious and that I would never see him again. I became angry at the thought, thinking she would find some way to keep me from him. I became angry with her. Even though he mistreated me, I felt like a woman with him. I enjoyed making him lose himself in me. I would consume him until he was drained and exhausted. He would sleep afterwards. It made me feel as if my job was well done.

Running Away

I began packing my clothes. I wanted to run away. I hid my bag in the closet. I tried to think of where I would go if I did run. I thought of my father. I remembered his name. I knew that would be the last place my mom would look for me.

I wrote him a letter, asking him why he wasn't in my life and to help me. I looked up his address in the phone book and sent the letter. Two weeks later, he called my aunt and told her to bring me over there.

He lived in another small town called Humboldt. My aunt took me to see him.

"Come on in," he said.

We walked into his house. He spent most of the time talking to my aunt. We talked a little. He, basically, told me that I couldn't stay with him and that he didn't know if I was his daughter or not. He was drunk when he slept with my mom. He did not remember finishing.

I was very disappointed when I left. I felt unwanted. I didn't think I would ever talk to him again. I felt like the result of a one-night stand. I had nowhere to go. I went home.

I decided to walk everyday. This became my way of running away from home daily. I walked all over town. I walked for at least two to three hours a day. I thought about what I could do, how to get Gregory off my mind, and stay away from home as much as possible.

No one ever looked for me, except Gregory. I continued sleeping with him. My brother even started taking me to meet him. At other times, I would get one of my friends to drop me off and pick me up later. I know my mom knew. I did not care. I loved him.

We began to talk a little. I told him about my episode with my father. He told me that his father wasn't in his life either. He told me that my father was really missing out. He didn't tell me what he meant by it. We just left it at that.

Months later, as my mom and I sat in the church parking lot, she questioned me.

"Are you still messing with him?"

"Yes."

"Even after I told you to stop?"

"I can't stop. I'm not going to."

I got out of the car. I thought she would hit me if I stayed in the car. As I walked to the choir, I wondered why it mattered to her. She was never home. When she was there, she was always on the phone. I had been sleeping with him for almost a year and she had only caught us once.

His sister and I were still friends, but I hadn't told her. She would be mad at me. She didn't like his attitude. Thus, she kept her distance from him.

I decided to tell her. It was summer again. Shauna had some thing for my brother. She began to come over more often than before. She sat on the floor in my room when I told her.

"Shauna, I got something to admit."

"What?"

"I've been messing with your brother for a while now."

"I know that. Everyone knows. I remember when he offered to take you home last summer. He's never done that to my friends."

"Why didn't you tell me you knew?"

"I was waiting for you to tell me. You should not be sleeping with him anyway. He's no good for you. He still messes with Sarah. He still sleeps with Karen sometimes too. He sleeps with everybody."

That lump came back. It hit hard. She stood and walked to my brother's room. I could hear the bed hitting the wall.

I didn't cry this time. I went walking. This was my method of releasing my depression, stress, and anger. In addition, it made me look and feel good. I had dropped six pant sizes. I was down to an eight. I wanted to get there by my junior year in High School. I made it.

When I got back to the house, my brother yelled, "Gregory is looking for you!"

I thought, *he has to have had enough of sleeping with me by now.*

I returned his call.

"Hello."

"Yeah, what's up?"

"Can I come and get you?"

"Yeah."

"Okay, I'm on my way."

We went to his house. I told him that I told Shauna about us.

"I'm sure she already knew."

"Why you say that?"

"A lot of people know. My mom asked me about it."

"Shauna told me to stop messing with you. She told me about the other girls. I know I should stop."

He grabbed me by my shoulders.

"You should stop listening to everybody else. That's what you should do."

"You're sleeping with everyone else."

"I'm with you everyday, Layla. Sometimes, I'm with you two and three times a day."

"Yeah, but, you still sleep with other girls. I'm still the girl you're sneaking around with."

"You're young. You're six years younger than me."

"So you can't be seen with me? You take those other girls out. What do you do for me? You grab food and bring it to the house."

We were quiet. He knew I was right. He hid me. I hated it.

I started working at McDonald's that summer. We didn't have a McDonald's in Atwood. We only had three gas stations and a small grocery store in our town. McDonald's was in the town in which Gregory lived. The position was okay. It was some funds in my pocket to pay for clothes. I told my mom I would pay the water bill to help her. My brother paid the cable bill. That gave her a little extra money.

Gregory picked me up from work sometimes. It felt so

good to see him. Some of my coworkers watched me get into his car. Everyone knew him. You could always hear him coming. He had fixed his car up. He had rims, a system, and fat tires on a Mercedes. Everyone knew his car. They would marvel at it, while I marveled at the driver. I didn't care about the car.

God's Saving Grace

I really don't know the true story behind the mishap. The story was changed so many times.

On April 18, 1996, I had awakened for school. Gregory had called last night at 11:40, wanting to meet me. My mom was home. Therefore, I couldn't.

I walked into the school. My friend Steve came over. His friends stood behind him, staring at me. I felt awkward.
"You doing okay?"
I sighed. "I feel a little sick."
"I bet. Man, I'm sorry for what happen to your boy this morning."
What is he talking about? I had no idea what was going on. Aware of my confusion, Steve continued, "Your boy Gregory got killed around one this morning."
"What?"
"Yeah, everybody's been talking about it."
"No, he didn't. I talked to him last night."
His friends began to agree with him.
I shook my head in disbelief. I couldn't think. I grabbed my backpack and headed to the phone. I called his number.
"Hello."
"May I speak to Gregory?"
"Ma'am now is not a good time."
The person on the other end hung up. I felt faint. I tried to maintain my composure. I stood in the hall trying to remember his tone last night before we hung up. He didn't seem as if anything was wrong. I walked to class, talking to God as I walked.

Everyone was checking on me throughout the day. I tried to hide my feelings, not believing what they were telling me. During lunch, I couldn't eat. Everyone watched, waiting for me to break down. I ran to the bathroom. My friend Leslie was behind me. I couldn't hold it anymore. I held my stomach, unable to hold in the pain. I knew something had happened.

"Tree, are you okay."

"I talked to him last night. He was fine. He was upset that I couldn't meet him. But, he was fine."

"Did you call?"

"Yes, some man answered and told me now wasn't a good time."

"Did he say that he was okay?"

"No, he hung up."

I cried. She stayed there with me. I knew she would. She knew I was in love with him. Losing him would have been more than I could bear.

My mom picked me up from school early. She was quiet until we were close to the house.

"I know why you're sick. I know what happened."

"Is he okay?"

"I don't think so. They said his body is on his porch."

"Who? Who said it?"

"Merrill told me."

"How does she know?"

"She said everyone is talking about it. I told you to leave him alone. He was nothing, but trouble."

"You don't know him."

"I know he wanted to go for bad."

We pulled into the yard. I ran to my room, locked the door, and hid my face in the pillow. I prayed. I prayed that what they were telling me wasn't true. I prayed that he was okay, that things would go back to normal once they realized it wasn't him.

I became angry with myself, thinking that things would have been different if he would have been with me last night. I fell asleep while I was praying and crying.

I woke up and called Shauna. I had to know the truth. I couldn't take it anymore, all of this the day before my prom.

"Hello."

"Shauna, what happened?" I was already crying again.

"Girl, I don't know. People are all over the place. The police are everywhere…."

"Is he okay?"

"I don't know. They won't tell us anything."

"Why? You're his sister."

"I know, but they're not answering any questions now. I gotta go. I'll call you when I find out what's going on. I can tell you that someone told me that it was him, someone told me it wasn't. I'll call you back."

I felt sick all over again. I didn't come out of my room until the next morning.

I went to school. I tried to avoid conversing with anyone. I knew that conversing with them would have caused me to break. I spoke briefly. I did promise my date that I was still going to the prom.

Getting ready for the prom was hard. I knew my hair was incredibly ridiculous. I didn't care. There was no one to impress. My heart was in pieces.

My date arrived in a limo. I jumped in. He looked at me in disgust.

"Did you shave your legs?"

"Yeah… Yesterday… The hairs grow back fast." That was the dumbest lie I had ever told anyone.

We arrived at the plaza. We took photos. We sat for about twenty minutes.

"Are you okay?"

"No."

"Do you want to go home?"

"Yes. I don't think I want to be here."

"The limo is still here. You go home. I'll get Chris to take me home."

"Are you sure?"

"Yeah, I can't imagine what you're going through."

I went home and headed straight for my room. My mom stopped me.

"What are you doing back?"

"I didn't feel good."

'I don't know what's wrong with you. Plus, some boy has been calling here, asking for you."

My heart raced. I grabbed the phone and dialed Gregory's number, praying for a miracle.

"Hey, baby."

I cried tears of joy hearing him, knowing he was alive. I was finally able to breathe.

"Are you okay?"

He laughed, "Yeah."

"I love you."

"I love you too."

"I'm sorry."

"For what?"

"For not letting you come and get me that night. You wouldn't have been there."

"Yeah, but you never know. God does things for a reason. You could have been hurt."

"I know, but God knows I love you. I love you more than you will ever know."

"Really?"

"Do you question that? You don't know how bad my heart has been hurting."

I wanted him to know everything. I had to get it all out. I never thought for a moment that my life would change as it did that day. After something that life threatening, now that I had the opportunity, I had to tell him. I wanted to see him so bad. I wanted to protect him, to cover his body with mine so that he would know that no pain would have been greater than to lose him. I loved him that much. I cried and talked.

When we hung up the phone, I thanked God over and over and over.

"You knew that would have been unbearable. Thank you!"

I slept.

The newspaper article about this incident came out the following Tuesday. The story stated that even though Gregory was unemployed, he owned a Mercedes. The headline stated that a jammed gun probably saved him. I say it was God's grace that spared him.

Gregory had to relocate. I waited over two months before I received my first call from him. My mom said to me, "I told you that he didn't give a damn about you. If a man really cares about you, he will call you."

We hardly ever saw each other after that incident. Almost every time I saw him, I cried. I cried with mixed emotions. Sad because I couldn't see or hear from him everyday. Happy, because he was alive.

A year after high school, I attended Tennessee State University. Gregory and I lived three hours away. Therefore, I was able to see more and more of him.

The Mishap

It was my second semester of college. I hadn't seen Gregory in two weeks. I craved him, longing to fall asleep beside him. I called.

"What's up?"

"Just thinking about you."

"What were you thinking?"

"I haven't seen you in two weeks and I want some so bad."

He chuckled, "You're crazy. You know that?"

"Crazy for you."

"It better be only me. Don't let me have to come down there."

"What are you going to do?"

"You know."

"What?"

"You'll see."

I couldn't wait. I couldn't take it anymore.

"Can I come and see you?"

"When?"

"Tonight. I don't have to work tomorrow."

"You'll have to come all the way."

"Okay! I'll leave in thirty minutes."

"Okay."

"Love ya."

"Love you, too."

I hung up. I felt like a kid on the way to Disneyland. I packed my clothes, debating on bringing pajamas. I knew they wouldn't stay on. I put on the tightest jeans and shirt that I had, ran my fingers through my hair, and left. I turned on my music as I was driving. I needed something to ease my anxiety.

Two hours forty-five minutes later, I called.

"What's up?"

"Hey, I'm about 10 miles from the Papermill Exit."

"I need you to meet me somewhere else. My friend Jordan's girl is out of town for the weekend and he wants us to stay at his place and keep him company."

"Okay."

I was a little disappointed because there were limits being that we were in someone else's home. He gave me the directions and we met. He got out of his car. All that I could think of was how amazing his body was. I opened my door, jumped out, and put my arms around him. He laughed. I was so happy to see him.

"Hey, Jordan is waiting on us."

"Okay."

"Get in and follow me."

"Why can't you ride with me?"

"You want me to?"

"Yes."

"Okay, I'll tell Jordan we're going to follow him."

He began to step away, but stopped. He turned back to me.

"By the way, you look so good. I can't wait."

I smiled.

"Thanks. I was thinking the same thing when you stepped out of his car. I want you right now, but I can wait til we get to his house."

He got in the car. We followed his friend. When we arrived, he took my bag and put it in a room. His friend watched me as I glared out of the window, making me uncomfortable. Gregory grabbed me around my waist. We kissed.

"You're so sexy."

"She sure is," said Jordan.

Gregory didn't flinch. It's as if he didn't care if his friend looked at me.

"I'm tired," I said. I lied, but I felt awkward.

"You want to lie down?"

"Yes."

We went to the room, closed the door, and went at it. He knew that I couldn't resist him. I lay on the bed. He unzipped my pants, pulled up my shirt, and kissed around my navel. I pulled him to me.

"I want you now."

28

He smirked. He loved teasing me, taking his time, sucking my toes, kissing my legs, working his way up until I was about to explode. It drove me insane.

He climbed on top of me, entered me, and gave me the high I longed for.

"You love me?" he asked.

"You know I do."

He walked to the bathroom, came back with a soapy towel, and cleaned me as if I was a baby. I was, his baby. We slept.

I woke up the next morning and realized I was in the bed alone. I threw on clothes and walked to the living room. Gregory was already dressed.

"What are you doing?"

"I'm hungry. I'm going to go to Waffle House. Do you want something?"

"Just a waffle."

"That's it?"

"Yeah."

"Okay, take a shower and I'll be back."

I could feel his friend watching.

"Hey, come here."

I pulled him to the couch.

"What?"

"Don't leave me here with him."

"Layla, that's my best friend. He won't bother you. I trust him."

"He makes me nervous."

He rubbed his hands through my hair, looked me in the eyes, and said, "I trust him."

He left. I went to take a shower.

I locked the door, but as I was in the shower, I heard the doorknob turning. I jumped out of the shower, pulled my shirt over my head, and tried to pull the bathroom drawer in front of the door. I was too late. His friend had already opened the door.

"What are you doing in here?"

"I have to pee."

"Did you have to pick the lock?"

He came closer to me.

"Please leave."

I was so afraid.

"You're so sexy."

"I thought you had to pee."

He pinned himself against me.

"Stop, please, stop."

He became angry and aggressive.

"No", I said while pushing him away.

"No one tells me no!" he exclaimed.

I sat on the toilet cover. He pushed his way between my legs, balled his fist, and shoved it in me. I was bleeding and crying. He picked me up and headed to the bedroom. I tried to grab the doorframe. He slammed me against his girlfriend's shoe rack. I tried to fight back. I didn't know what he was going to do to me. He threw me on the bed. I continued struggling and screaming. Finally, the neighbor heard me. It startled him. I kneed him in the private and ran. I grabbed my clothes from the bathroom and headed for the door. Jordan was guarding the door.

"You can't leave."

Honestly, I don't remember everything that was said. I do remember that I agreed not to go to the police. Before letting me leave, Jordan told me that Gregory did not go to the Waffle House. Instead, he went to check on his girlfriend that he was living with.

My heart was crushed, but I was happy to be alive. I stopped at a phone booth and dialed 911. The operator answered.

"What procedures do I have to take when someone has tried to rape me?"

"You have to come in and fill out a form. Then, you will be examined. Whatever you do, don't shower."

30

"Okay."

I hung up. I walked back to my car. Everything was going through my head. I contemplated on going to the police. I thought of everything I would go through after I pressed charges against Jordan. I thought of how many times he apologized for what he did, while I sat on his sofa crying. I thought of Gregory and how he left me there, wondering if he set me up. I wondered if Gregory really believed that, by him not being there, I would sleep with his best friend. I wondered if Gregory ever really loved me or even thought enough of me to not put me in that kind of situation. I had no answer. I sat in my car, crying. It was hard for me to believe what had happened to me. Nevertheless, I felt it. My underwear had blood drippings. The blood had stained my pants. I had evidence. I drove back to the dorm.

My roommate was gone when I got to the room. I changed clothes, lied in the bed, and cried myself to sleep. When I got up, she was there.

"Why are you in bed so early?"

"I'm not feeling well."

"Why, what's wrong with you?"

"Nothing, I just don't feel well."

She didn't say anything. She headed for the shower. Once again, I thought of Jordan and Gregory. I realized that I was unable to testify against him. I wasn't ready to put anyone in jail. I was also afraid that I would find out that Gregory had set me up. That would have hurt me more than anything Jordan could have ever done to me. I had put my pants and underwear in a bag just in case I ever whipped up some courage.

I was weak and felt filthy. I grabbed my robe and headed for the shower. As I showered, I cried. I hadn't thought of eating. I couldn't. I headed back to the room to rest.

I woke up the next day. I felt weaker. I decided not to go to work. I called and told them I wasn't feeling well. I tried to think of someone I could trust with not repeating what happened. I called Shauna.

"Hello."

"Hey."

"What's wrong with you?"

I began to cry. "Shauna, please don't tell anyone."

"What happened?"

"You have to promise."

"What happened?"

"Promise."

"Okay, I promise."

"Jordan tried to rape me."

She was silent. "Where was Gregory?"

"He told me he was going to get us something to eat."

"Did he ever come back?"

"I don't know. I didn't stay."

I told her everything that I could remember.

"I bet Gregory set you up."

"Why?"

"Gregory doesn't care about anyone, but Gregory."

"He's your brother."

"Yeah, and I told you to leave him alone a long time ago."

"I know, but I love him."

"He set you up to get raped!"

I could tell Shauna was angry. She talked to me about pressing charges against Jordan and Gregory. I told her I couldn't. I was just relieved to be able to tell someone.

I didn't go to class on Monday. I stayed in bed most of the day. I only got out of bed to shower. I still felt dirty. I had not eaten anything since Friday. I felt really weak. I dodged my roommate as much as possible. I needed to be alone.

Later that evening, I dressed and went to get something to eat. Instead of eating, I stopped at Exxon and grabbed a drink. Later that night, I ate a salad.

The next day, I attended all of my classes. I went back to the room, completed my homework, changed clothes, and headed for work.

32

After work, I went back to the campus. My roommate was sitting on her bed.

"Your mom has been calling you."

"Okay. I'll call her in the morning."

She was watching me.

"What's going on with you? I haven't seen you. You haven't been eating with us. You look like you're not even eating."

"I'm just going through something. That's all. I'll be okay."

I tried not to cry, but the tears were already coming. I wiped my face, grabbed the phone, and sat in the hallway outside of my room to call my mom.

"Hello."

"Hey Ma."

"Tree, Shauna called me today. I already knew because Jordan's mom came to me and apologized for what he had done."

I began to cry.

"It's your brother," she said. "You better call and talk to him. He told me he would kill Jordan. You talk to him. I tried, but he is so mad."

I managed an "Okay". I immediately called my brother.

"Hey."

"Tree, are you okay."

"Yeah, I'm okay."

"Where does he live?"

"Please don't do anything stupid."

"You are my sister, my little sister. Do you know how much you mean to me?"

"Yes, but he's not worth it."

"You're my best friend. I don't want anyone hurting you."

"I know."

We talked. I told him what happened and why I didn't go to the police.

"Have you talked to Gregory?"

"No, I don't want to."

"Has he called?"

"No."

That made him angrier. We talked until he was calm. I told him that I loved him.

I called my mom back. She told me that Jordan had told his mom what he had done and that he may have to spend time in jail. I don't know why, but I felt sorry for him. Everything felt awkward. I hang up with my mom, showered, and lied down. Then, the phone rang again. I thought my mom was calling again.

"Hello."

"What happened?"

It was Gregory. I wanted to hang up, but couldn't. I wanted to know if he had set me up. I wanted to know about the other woman. I wanted to know everything.

"Why did you really leave me?"

"I went to get something to eat. When I came back, you were gone. I asked Jordan where you had gone. He said home. I asked what happened. He said that he tried to sleep with you, you said no, and left."

He didn't seem angry about Jordan trying to sleep with me. I sat in disbelief at the fact that his best friend tried to sleep with me and he seemed to be okay with it. Almost five years of my life and my boyfriend still didn't love me. That hurt. I tried to abandon the thought, but couldn't. We talked a while longer before hanging up.

Our relationship was very rocky after that happened. Deep down, I knew we wouldn't stay together. I needed someone different. I knew it. I longed for someone that respected me and treated me like royalty. I needed a change.

Greener Grass

It was August 1999. I was working at Amoco, usually from 10 p.m. to 6 a.m.. I liked this shift because it wasn't anywhere near as busy as the other shifts. I worked in a small, closed-in booth because the store was in the hood. We made almost all of our money off beer, cigarettes, and gas.

One day, I had walked out of the building to assist an elderly woman with the pump. I felt someone staring. I looked around as I was walking back into the building. That's when I spotted him. He had just pulled up. His stare was vicious, almost uncomfortable. I knew that he would say something to me. I looked his way again as I walked past his car. He fingered for me to come to him. I walked over.

"What's up?"

"You."

His lips were perfect, wet from him licking them as I walked by.

"Do you have any kids?"

(I had to ask. I had met so many guys in that area that had several. I didn't want the drama. I had no kids of my own and was not ready to take care of anyone else's. I knew I would have walked away if he said yes.)

He shook his head as if to say "no".

"How old are you?"

"Twenty-three."

I thought to myself, *Twenty-three, nice lips, no kids, no braids, no gold teeth, no signs of homosexuality, and he wasn't high. Perfect.* I already had a boyfriend. I took his number with intentions of hooking him up with my friend Yanna.

"By the way, what's your name?"

"Delante."

It fit him. I figured I would converse with him, find out what kind of person he is, and decide on whether or not to hook them up.

Yanna was a thick, red-bone with a beautiful personality and long hair. She considered her height her downfall. I thought Delante would have been great for her. I figured I would call him the next day and drill him with questions. I had to work the second shift Saturday. I decided I would call him from there.

I called him while I was at work doing absolutely nothing.

"Hello."

"Hey!"

"Who is this?"

"Layla."

"Who?"

"The girl that you met at the gas station yesterday."

"Ahh, what's up?"

"Nothing. Are you busy?"

"Naw, chilling with my homeboys."

"Hey. Can you sing?"

"No, you wanna hear me?"

"Yeah."

Delante began to sing. His singing was horrible. I use to visualize my husband singing to me and rubbing his hands through my hair while I lay on him. Delante's ruckus was not the vision. I was sure that I would hook him up with Yanna. He was definitely not for me.

After singing, he asked, "What time are you getting off?"

"Ten. Why? What's up? Wanna see me?"

"Yeah, I'll be up there when you get off."

"Alright."

He pulled up at ten. My relief hadn't made it. He called.

"What's up?"

"My relief isn't here yet."

"Did you call her?"

"No. If you want, you can come in."

"Okay. Open the door."

He got out of the car and came in.

"Can I get a drink?"

"Yeah, I'll pay for it."

He grabbed the drink. We started talking. A few minutes later, my relief arrived. She spoke to both of us. I told him I would be out in a minute. He, then, went to his car.

"Are you talking to him?"

"No, but he's cute. I told him I had a boyfriend. So, we're just cool."

"Okay, just to let you know he's going with Kelsey's cousin."

"Really? He told me he didn't have a girlfriend."

"He's lying. She's crazy too. So, you don't want to go there."

"Okay."

He was still in the parking lot when I headed to my car.

"Hey."

"Yeah."

"Follow me."

I followed him. We stopped in an empty parking lot in front of a business complex. I got out of my car and into his. He smiled as if he were happy to see me. I thought of what my coworker said.

"Hey, did you know my coworker?"

"Yeah, a little."

"She told me that you have a girlfriend."

"I don't. She's not my girl. I just can't get her to leave me alone."

"Oh."

I figured that he really didn't have a reason to lie to me. Therefore, I changed the subject.

We talked for a while. We talked about my boyfriend, school, and anything else we could think to discuss. He was really cool. We agreed we would be friends. I discussed my friend, Yanna, and the possibilities of hooking them up. He told me that he would like to meet her.

It was so great to talk to him. I felt relieved to be able to discuss so many things with him. Hours had gone by. I needed to get back to the school. We agreed to meet again.

The next day, I went to class. I was tired afterwards. I decided to lie down. I had two hours before my next class.

That's when the phone rang.

"Hello."

"Who is this?"

"Layla."

"Do you know JD?"

"No."

I kind of figured this was the girl he had told me about. I figured I would just deny everything so that she would stop calling.

"He drives an Expedition."

"I don't know him."

"I found your number in his phone. He called you last night."

"He called the wrong number."

"Okay."

"Okay."

I thought about the phone call for a minute. I decided I would say something to him about it when I talked to him.

I went to work at two. About fifteen minutes later, Delante pulled up. He motioned for me to let him in.

"Hey."

"What's up?"

He hugged me really tight: like he hadn't seen me in a while.

"Nothing," I said as I chuckled about the hug. I thought about the call.

"Oh yeah, today, some girl called my phone asking about a guy named "JD". She said he drives an expedition. Is that your girl?"

"That's the girl I can't get rid of."

"How'd she get your phone? Well, it doesn't matter."

"I'm sorry she called you. It will never happen again."

By the way he looked, I believed him. We chat for a little while longer.

"Hey, you want to go bowling tomorrow night?"

"We can. I don't get off until ten again."

"That's fine. One of my homeboys will probably go with us. You got a friend for him?"

"Yeah, I'll ask this girl in my class tomorrow. She's cool."

"Is she cute?"

"Yeah."

"Alright. I'm going to get something to eat. Are you hungry?"

"No. I'm fine."

"Okay. I'll see you later."

The next night, we went bowling. We also spent some time at the arcade. I felt like a kid in the arcade. The two we brought with us seemed to have fun also. Delante kissed me while we were in the arcade. I did not stop him. It felt so good. Moreover, I liked the way his eyes danced when we were around each other.

The next night, I had to work the late shift. I went in at ten. I had talked to Delante earlier. He told me that he would come by to see me at work. When I saw his car, I ran to crack the door so that he could come in. I heard the door open.

"Hey!"

"Hey."

It wasn't his voice. I looked towards the back. His friend that was with us at the bowling alley was standing there.

"Oh, I thought you were Delante."

"No."

"What's up?"

"Delante is not who you think he is."

"Really?"

"Yeah."

"Is he not your friend?"

"We're cool."

"Are you driving his car?"

"No, that's my car. We both have gold Hondas."

"Did you come here to tell me about him?"

"Not really. I came here to tell you that I really like you. I think you're beautiful. We should start spending time together."

"Did he tell you that I have a boyfriend?"

"No."

"I do. So, I can't talk to either of you."

"You should just give me a try."

"I'm okay."

We chat a little while longer. I thought that Delante knew about what was happening; trying to see what kind of girl I am. I had just talked to him. It seemed odd that his friend was standing here, confessing his interest in me. It was also hard to believe that they both had the same kind of car.

His friend left. As he pulled off, I wrote his tag number on a sheet of paper. About five minutes later, Delante pulled up. I made sure it was him this time.

"Hey!"

"Hey!"

He hugged me. His eyes were dancing. I chuckled a little.

"What?"

Nothing."

I could not tell him his eyes told everything.

"Did you send your friend here?"

"Who?"

"The guy that was with us last night."

"No. He was here?"

He looked startled.

"Yes, I thought it was you because of the car. So, I cracked the door, waiting for you to step in."

"Yeah, we have cars alike. He bought his before me. What did he want?"

I told him everything that we had talked about, watching his expression as I talked. He seemed upset.

I knew Delante was starting to like me. Honestly, I liked spending time with him too. When I was with him, my problems with Gregory didn't exist. As far as I knew, Gregory was still sleeping around on me. I didn't care anymore. I was tired of being unhappy.

Delante and I talked for hours. We shared a few kisses in the process. I thought about Yanna, feeling guilty about kissing the guy I'm supposed to be hooking her up with. She hadn't even met him.

40

His kisses were soft and smooth. I didn't want to stop. As our breathing hardened, I would stop us, not wanting to go too far. I totally ignored the warning from his friend, thinking he only told me those things to get in good with me. In addition, I was still with Gregory.

Delante and I had started spending almost everyday together. He would drive up to my dorm as I was walking from class. He had learned my schedule. Therefore, he always knew when I was getting out of class. I loved the time we were spending together. There were no strings attached. In addition, he was always there, comforting me after my arguments with Gregory, shopping with me, taking me out to places I hadn't heard of. He made me feel good about myself. He restored that esteem Gregory had destroyed. When we were together, I didn't have to pretend to be anyone else. I felt that I could finally love being me.

Gregory came down for homecoming. I had told Delante the day before. He was really upset about it.
"I wanted to spend time with you."
"I want to spend time with you too, but my friends from home are coming too. We're all going out as couples."
"So, what if I found someone else to hang out with while you're with him?"
I felt a lump in my throat.
"I couldn't say anything to you. This is my boyfriend. I can't just tell him that he can't come so I can be with you. How would that sound?"
He walked away. I wanted to grab him. I hated that I wouldn't be able to see him.

Homecoming night, my friend, Leslie, and her boyfriend, my brother and his girlfriend, and Gregory and I went out to eat. As we were finishing, Gregory asked my brother to take me back to the hotel so that he could go out with his cousin.

I asked, "You're not going bowling with us?"

"No, I promised T that I would hang out with him."

"Oh."

On the way back to the hotel, my brother told me I was stupid. He laughed about Gregory leaving me at the hotel. I walked in the room and cried, thinking about how much fun I could have been having with Delante.

Gregory came in early the next morning. He turned me over for sex. It was horrible. I was so disgusted with him. I tried to tell him that I was humiliated with how he had left me to go hang out with his cousin. He told me to shut-up. I didn't argue back. I let him sleep, thinking of how I could make things up to Delante.

Everyone left the next morning. I was glad. I was afraid to call Delante. I knew he was upset. I decided to wait for him to call me.

I went to work at ten. He pulled up. He watched me as he was getting out of the car. I looked towards him. He seemed upset, but motioned for me to let him in. I almost ran to the door. We didn't say much. We kissed liked we hadn't seen each other in years. It felt so good. He held me close to him as I wrapped my arms around him. Then, he pushed me away from him.

"Did you sleep with him?"

"Of course, he's my boyfriend. He would expect something if I didn't."

He was disappointed.

"Honestly, it was horrible. Everything was horrible."

I tried to get off the subject of Gregory.

"So, what did you do?" I asked.

"My boys and I hung out."

"Really, did you have fun?"

"It was cool."

He didn't say much more. We talked for a while. I told him how Gregory had humiliated me. He seemed a little relieved that I didn't have fun.

I was really starting to open up to Delante. I spent more and more time at his house. One day, as I was looking through the pictures he had hanging on the wall; I noticed writing on the bottom of one of the photos. It was a photo of Delante and a little boy. It had "I Love My Dad" at the bottom of the photo. I saw another photo of him with another name at the bottom of it. I headed towards the door. He was right behind me.

"Where are you going?"

"Home."

"Why?"

"I just saw that picture of you and that little boy. I thought you didn't have any kids. Plus, there was another photo of you with another name on it. Who in the hell is Jason?"

He sighed.

"That's my real name."

"Why did you tell me that it was Delante?"

"Because I had to change my name in order to receive my father's inheritance when he died."

"So you had to change your name to receive the house and the cars?"

"Yes."

"What about the little boy?"

"That's my son."

"You told me you didn't have any kids."

I got into my car. Everything he was saying seemed bogus. As I was getting ready to pull off, he sat on the ground, putting his legs under my car.

"Can you move?"

"No, please talk to me."

I put my car in drive.

"Are you just going to run over me?"

"Why did you lie to me?"

"I didn't think our relationship would go this far."

"You still didn't have to lie to me."

"Would you have talked to me if I told you the truth?"

"Probably not."

"Exactly. That's why I didn't tell you."

"I was honest with you. I told you I had a boyfriend."

"I know. I know. I'm sorry."

"How many kids do you have?"

"One."

"One?"

"Yes."

"You could have told me that."

"I know. I'm sorry. Will you please turn the car off?"

I turned my car off. He opened the door and pulled me out.

"I'm really sorry."

"You don't have to lie to me, Delante. Jason. I don't even know what to call you. Maybe I'll just call you JD."

"I know. Look at me. I'm really, really sorry."

He pulled me close.

"No more lies," I demanded.

"Okay."

I ended my relationship with Gregory on November 2, 1999. It wasn't as hard for me now that JD and I were spending so much time together. Besides, I was really enjoying our time. There never seemed to be a dull moment. I hadn't seen Gregory since September. I didn't have a desire to see him. I loved the way JD made me feel.

My friend, Chase was coming to Nashville for her birthday. I told her we could go out to one of the clubs. I wasn't familiar with all of them. Therefore, I asked JD if he would take us.

On our way to the club, we stopped by the liquor store to purchase some vodka. I mixed our drinks as JD was driving. We reached 2nd Avenue when JD stopped at the light. His foot was on the brake. His head was on the steering wheel. I put the car in park. Chase and I got out and put JD in the back seat. I drove him back to his house. Chase and I helped him into the house. Then, I took Chase back to the hotel.

"Sorry we didn't quite make it into the club. I had no idea he was that intoxicated."

"It's okay. I still had fun. JD is cute."

"You think so?"

"Yeah, I think he likes you."

"I don't know. We're cool. He's fun to hang around, but I don't know."

"Well, I'll see ya."

"Okay. I'll see ya later."

I headed back to JD's to see if he was okay. He was upstairs asleep. I needed a way back to the dorm. I awakened him.

"Are you okay?"

"Yeah. I'm alright."

"I need to get back to the dorm. Will you be able to drive back here?"

"Come here."

JD pulled me towards him.

"I'm sorry we didn't get to go out."

"It's okay. I think she was a little intoxicated herself. She had already drank Crown at the hotel with her other friends."

"Can you just stay here tonight?"

"I don't know."

"Please, just come and lay with me. I don't want to sleep alone."

"Are you okay?"

"Yeah, I'm fine. I just want you to stay."

"Okay, but, I'm keeping my clothes on."

"That's fine."

I lied down in the bed. He pulled me to him, holding me like a teddy. We slept.

In the middle of the night, I awoke. JD was kissing all over me.

"Maybe I should leave."

"Please don't."

He spoke softly.

"You're intoxicated."

"I'm not. Layla, I really enjoy our time together. Right now, I just want to please you."

"I don't know. I just broke up with Gregory two weeks ago."

I wanted him. I didn't want him to know. I should have left earlier. Then, I wouldn't be debating on whether or not to give into him. I stopped JD's kisses to get his attention.

"JD, I don't want our relationship to change."

"It won't."

"No, really, I really enjoy our time together. I have so much fun with you."

JD was running his hands up and down my back, kissing around my waist as he took off my shirt. His eyes were dancing. Heat was rising in me as he touched me, using his fingertips. I gasped for breath. The air was cold, but our bodies were warm against each other. JD pulled my legs open as I lay on the bed. He headed downward. I grabbed the sheets to gain control of myself. He pulled himself upward, moving into me slowly. He gasped as he entered me. He moved back immediately, shaking his head as if he couldn't handle it.

He reentered me, taking his time, trying to move slowly to prolong himself. It didn't last. He gasped, burying his head in the sheets, trying to fight himself.

I was almost there; tears were already rolling down the sides of my face.

"Don't stop."

"I can't help it."

"I'm almost there."

He was pouting, trying to fight it. I softly grasped his butt, pushing him in as I came. He did the same while pulling out. We lay in the dark on the sheets, damp from our orgasms. His head was in the crease of my stomach. We slept.

At some time that night, JD had awakened, thrown the sheets off the bed, and pulled the comforter over us. When I woke the next morning, he was holding me. His body was soft against mine. I lay there, thinking about what was going to come of us. I didn't want the fun I was having to end. Slowly, I pushed away from him, having to go to the bathroom. As I stood, I felt his hand around my wrist. I jumped.

"Where are you going?"

"To the bathroom."

"Oh. Make sure you come back."

I didn't reply. I didn't expect him to wake. Therefore, I was surprised when he grabbed me.

I washed my hands and happily returned to his bed. He smiled as if he had been waiting.

"Come here."

We started all over again.

JD and I began to see each other almost daily. I had started spending the night with him. During my fall break, I stayed at a hotel so I could continue working and spending time with him. He stayed there with me almost every night. Gregory had not accepted the fact that I was no longer with him. Therefore, he still called to argue with me.

One night, JD asked if I would like to go to the club with him.

"Yeah, I'll go."

"Okay, I'll pick you up around twelve."

"How old do I have to be to get in?"

"Twenty-one."

"I'm twenty."

"I know. Can't you get your sister's ID?"

"Yeah, I'll get it."

JD didn't show until one that morning. I was a little upset from waiting.

"Why are you so late?"

"I got tied up. I'm sorry."

"Why didn't you call?"

"I'm sorry."

"I don't want to go now."

"Why?"

"Because, I'm a little sleepy."

I sat on the bed. He sat on the other bed, facing me.

"Layla, I'm really sorry. I do want to take you."

"I didn't get my sister's ID."

"I'll take you to get it."

"Why do you want me to go so bad?"

He sighed, "When I'm with you, none of my problems exist. I really enjoy spending time with you. You're cool, funny, goofy….."

"Shut-up."

We laughed. I gave in. We headed to my sister's to get her ID. When we pulled up, my sister was at the door. I grabbed her ID and headed back to the car before she started fussing at me for coming over late.

"Hey, I know him."

I stopped. "Do you?"

"Yeah, I used to work with him at the Sub."

"He still works there."

"You don't want him. He's trouble."

"We're friends."

"Okay, I'm just making sure."

"Yeah, that's it."

I headed back to the car, disappointed about what she had said. I got in the car as she shut her door.

"Do you know her?"

"She looks familiar."

"She told me she used to work with you at the Sub."

"Yeah, we did."

"She said you're trouble."

"Do you think so?"

"I don't know. You've lied to me about so much and…..."

"Okay, okay."

We free-styled on the way to the club. It was lame, but fun. When we arrived, the place was crowded. He shook hands with some of his friends at the door. When we finally got inside, we went straight to the dance floor. At some time, he left. I started dancing with other guys. When I was tired, I went to look for him. I couldn't find him anywhere. I walked outside.

As I walked out, he was coming in.

"Are you ready to go", I asked.

"Yeah, in a minute. Let's go back in."

"Why?"

"Well, we don't have to."

He grabbed my hand and headed towards the car. His phone was ringing. There was a girl blocking his car. She didn't look happy. I turned to go back.

"I'll go back in. I don't want any problems."

"No, I'll get her to move."

"I don't want any drama. I'll just go back in the club."

"No, let's just get in the car."

The girl got out as we were getting in the car. They began to argue. He was telling her to move her car so that we could leave.

"Where are you going?" she asked.

"I'm taking her home."

"Let me go with you."

"No."

"I'm not moving."

"You're not going with us."

They continued arguing. I couldn't take the back and forth. She was very upset.

"JD, she can ride with us. It's no biggie. You're just taking me home. As a matter of fact, I'll sit in the back."

I sat in the back seat. He looked at me as if I were crazy. She jumped in the front. He told her to get out and move her car. When she moved, he pulled off. She began to follow us. Somehow, we lost her. He stopped. I got in the front.

"Who was that?"

"This girl I used to talk to."

"Used to?"

"Yeah."

I shook my head.

"I don't want any connection to you."

He laughed, "Why?"

"You have too much drama."

As we reached the hotel, we became silent.

"Can I stay with you tonight?"

"No, I've had enough for tonight."

He laughed. I waved as I shut the door. I sighed. The feeling of loneliness set in. I was a little upset with him for that episode, but I refused to let him know. Besides, we were just friends.

I sat in my bed, debating on whether or not to ever call him again. The sex was great, but not worth the drama. I tried to reason that I could just sleep with him until I got into another relationship. I convinced myself not to expect more.

We became each other's stress reliever. The sex continued, everywhere. I thought everything was fine now that I knew who he really was.

One day in April, I was at his house. We headed to his room and, for a moment, I blacked out. Luckily, he was behind me.

"Are you okay?"

"I think so. I feel a little dizzy. Maybe I just need to sit down."

He sighed as I sat on the bed.

"Hey, we need to talk."

"I turned to look at him, confused by his look."

"About what?"

"We'll talk later."

"About what?"

He didn't reply. I left his house, headed to school, thinking about what he needed to talk to me about.

As I was walking to class, the dizzy spell returned. I felt sick all of a sudden. I was trying to remember what I had eaten that would make me sick. After my class, I walked to the campus health center. I told the nurse my symptoms.

"Wait here while I grab a pregnancy test."

"For what!"

"You're having all of the symptoms of someone that's pregnant."

"I may have a virus, but I'm not pregnant."

"Just take the test anyway."

I became angry with her, thinking to myself, *this heifer has the nerve to tell me I may be pregnant.*
She came back with the test.
"Here you go. Just go in that bathroom and urinate on this."
I wanted to snatch that pregnancy test right out of her hand. I went to the bathroom, urinated on the test, and waited to hear her tell me that she was wrong.
"Just as I thought. You're pregnant."
I closed my eyes; anger was building in me.
"That test is wrong! I can't be pregnant."
"Are you having sex?"
"Yes."
"Are you using protection?"
"No, but he hasn't done anything in me."
"You're pregnant."
She walked away. I was furious. I went to the hospital to get a second opinion.

The doctor came into the room at the hospital after they had run a few tests.
"Ma'am you have a cist on your ovaries that has began to burst. That's why you see little specks of blood every now and then."
I thought to myself *I knew she was wrong about me being pregnant. That woman was crazy.*
I was getting ready to leave when he said, "You're also two months pregnant."
I held my head down, "Two months."
"Yes ma'am."
"Thank you."

I was devastated. I couldn't believe he had gotten me pregnant after I had told him I wasn't ready for any kids. I left the hospital.

When I arrived at the school, I went to my room and lie in the bed, thinking about my messy situation. My roommate walked in.
"What's wrong with you?"
"I'm pregnant."

"What? By Gregory?"

"No, JD."

"Are you serious?"

"Yes. I haven't slept with Gregory in a while because I was sleeping with JD."

"Are you going to have the baby?"

"I'm going to take responsibility for my actions."

"Man, and you were supposed to hook him up with Yanna."

"I know."

"Have you told him?"

"I think he already knows. He told me he had to talk to me."

"You think he did it on purpose?"

"Kind of. I told him I wasn't ready for kids."

"Dang."

"Yeah, I know."

She headed for class. I decided to take a nap. As, I was dozing off, the phone rung.

"Hello."

"Hey. What are you doing right now?"

"I'm going to take a nap until my next class."

"What are you going to do after class?"

"Probably grab something to eat."

"Can I see you tonight? I need to talk to you."

"Yeah, I need to talk to you too."

"Alright, I'll pick you up after class."

I couldn't concentrate during class, thinking about my pregnancy. I was upset that he was so careless. I was with my ex-boyfriend for almost six years and never got pregnant. Why JD? I contemplated everything, wondering how much he would help me with this situation. The more I thought about it, the angrier I became. I began to blame JD for the whole situation. I decided to let him go. He was no good for me.

JD was waiting in front of my dorm as I came from class.

"Hey."

"Hey."

52

"Have you eaten yet?"

"No. I was getting ready to head over to the Sub."

"Get in and we can go get something to eat."

I got in the car. We headed to a restaurant. I was quiet. He was watching me.

"How was class?"

"It was okay."

"You're quiet."

"I know. I just have some things on my mind."

When we arrived at the restaurant, JD got out to open the door for me. I began to feel a little dizzy as I was getting out. I knew I needed to eat a little.

As we waited on our food, we began to chat.

"I know what you need to talk to me about."

"I'm sure you do."

"I'm sorry. It's just.....sometimes the sex was too good to stop. I did pull out, but after I had left a little."

"So, you would pull out after leaving some in me? You told me you pulled out every time!"

"I know. I did, but I would leave a little."

"Why?"

"Because I didn't want to stop."

I became angry. *How could he be so careless?*

"I'm ready to go."

"You don't want to eat."

"I don't feel like eating."

"Just grab something."

I wanted to grab him. I folded my arms. I didn't want everyone in the restaurant to see that I was angry. We ate and left.

While we were in the car, I said, "You make me feel like you did this on purpose. We both said we weren't ready for kids. You already have one."

He was silent. When we pulled up to the dorm, I got out and went to my room. I didn't want to talk to JD. I just needed time to think things over.

I didn't call him at all for two days. As I was working,

he pulled up. He motioned for me to let him in. I opened the door.

"What's up?"

"Nothing."

"You feeling okay?"

"I'm fine."

"Can you come over when you get off?"

"Why?"

"I want to talk to you."

It was Saturday. I had worked the 6 a.m. to 2p.m. shift.

"Why can't you just talk to me now?"

"Because I want to talk with no interruptions."

"I'll come over."

"As soon as you get off?"

"As soon as I get off."

He left.

As I pulled up, there were a lot of guys standing around. I called him.

"Hello."

"I'm not coming in there!"

"Why not?"

"Do you see all of these people outside?"

"Just come in."

"Can't you just get in the car and talk to me?"

"Come in."

"Come and get me."

"Okay."

He walked out to my car. There was a guy standing in the front yard putting cocaine in his nose with his pinky finger.

"You've got a crack head in your front yard."

"That's my brother."

"Are you serious?"

"Yeah."

I thought, my kid is going to have a crack head for an uncle.

We walked into the house. His friend, Montrell, stood

in the front room as if he was waiting for us.

"Hey!" I said to Montrell.

"Hey, what's up?"

"Nothing."

"You don't look pregnant."

"Hopefully not."

"How far along are you?"

"Only two months."

"Don't get big."

"I don't think that's avoidable."

"Just don't get big."

He walked out of the house. I looked at JD.

"What was that about?"

"I don't know."

"Okay, what do you want to talk to me about?"

"Come sit."

I sat on the loveseat with him. He grabbed my hands and looked at me with all sincerity.

"I love you."

I was rather shocked by that comment. I think he noticed.

"I do. If I could spend everyday with you, I would. I want a family with you, but right now is not a good time. I don't really think we should have this kid."

I thought, *no wonder he just told me he loves me.*

"I really thought about this myself. I don't think I could live with taking my kid's life. We discussed this before. I told you that we didn't believe in abortions. I told you I didn't want any kids right now either. That doesn't mean you should nut in me. Now you're telling me to have an abortion?"

"I just wanted to say we had something together."

"An abortion? That's insane. Is that why you told me you love me?"

"No, I meant that."

"Yeah, okay."

     I was tired. I knew he was lying again. I got up and walked out. I had friends that had abortions. I didn't want to be in that category. They always seemed like they had lost something. Like their joy was taken from them. It was a hard decision. To me, having an abortion was a way of saying, "I can't take responsibility for my actions."

We were cool, but JD was a liar. Therefore, I just decided to leave him alone and take care of my responsibility myself. I quit calling him. We didn't talk for days, but everyday that I worked, he came to get gas. I knew it wasn't for gas. Who buys gas daily?

Gregory's Visit

I was at work one night, studying, when the phone rang.

"Hello."

"Layla."

It was Gregory. I really wasn't in the mood for arguing with Gregory. I was arguing with JD earlier.

"Yeah."

"I miss you."

"Gregory, I'm working right now. I really don't feel like talking."

"I am going on a cruise and I want you to go."

"I can't."

"Why?"

"Gregory, I'm pregnant."

He became quiet.

"By who?"

"A guy named JD."

"So you've been whoring around?"

I wanted to snap. How could he?

"It's whatever you want to call it."

"You're a whore."

"Thank you."

I hung up. I began to think about everything that he had put me through. How good I was to him in spite of everything he had done to me. He cheated the whole time I was with him. Now, I'm a whore. I began to blame Gregory for my problems with JD, thinking *maybe if he had treated me right, this would have never happen.*

The next day, I called my father.

"Hello."

"Hey!"

"I haven't heard from you in a long time."

"I know."

"How are you?"

"I'm pregnant."

He was silent.

"I'm having so many problems right now. My ex is upset, calling me a whore, and the guy I'm pregnant by is off and on about my pregnancy."

"What do you mean?"

"One minute he wants me to have an abortion, the next minute he's excited about having a kid. I'm confused about the whole thing."

"Why are you confused?"

"Because, I don't want to have a kid, but I also feel that I should take responsibility for my actions. Neither JD nor Gregory is right for me. Sometimes, I really feel that if you would have been in my life like you were supposed to be, I would have never made such bad choices."

"Why do you feel that way?"

"Because if my father was there, he would have told me the kind of men that I wouldn't want in my life. Because you weren't, I chose these idiots."

He remained quiet. I hung up. I thought about what I had just said to him. At that time, everything made sense to me. I didn't realize that I was blaming everyone else for my actions except myself.

Gregory hadn't called me to argue anymore after I told him I was pregnant. He actually showed up at the gas station to see for himself. He walked over to the booth as I was checking out a customer. He motioned for me to let him in. I debated, but let him in anyway.

"What are you doing here?"

"I came to see if you were lying to me."

"About being pregnant?"

"Yes."

"I wouldn't tell you that if I wasn't."

He became angry when I pulled up my smock.

"How far along are you?"

"Almost six months."

He was trying to calculate to see if I was pregnant by him.

"As much I don't want it to be, I know I'm pregnant by JD."

"Who is JD?"

"This guy that lied to me about his whole life."

"So, you're pregnant by someone you're not going to be with?"

"Yeah."

"You're a whore and you're stupid."

"Did you come here to tell me all of this? If so, you could have just called."

He was sad. Tears began to roll down his face.

"I never thought you would ever do something like this to me. I trusted you more than I trusted my own mother."

I became angry with him. I started yelling.

"I can't believe you did a lot of stuff to me! I was faithful to you! I would have bent over backwards for you, but you never treated me right! You always cheated!"

I began to cry. The tension in the room was so strong. We were both upset. He stood with his fist balled. I backed away. He walked out.

I began to focus more on school and saving my money. I knew I had a rough road ahead. I began to buy diapers and everything that I thought I would need to prepare myself for this child. I read everyday, thinking it would make my baby smarter. I finally told my family. My younger cousin was pregnant also. So, my pregnancy wasn't a big deal. I was twenty. She was sixteen. All of the commotion was about her.

JD would take me out every now and then. We began to have more and more problems. I told him there were plenty of guys to date. That didn't play over well with him. He would see cars on campus and swear the owners were with me. The funny thing is I didn't know the guys that drove the cars. He started accusing me of everything under the sun. I thought he was insane.

On our way out for dinner one night, he asked, "How far along are you now?"

"Six months, almost seven."

He was quiet for a minute.

"I can't help you take care of your kid. I have kids myself."

"I thought you had one."

He reached into his glove compartment. He pulled out four photos and handed them to me. I looked through them. I was angry, but my sister had warned me three months ago that he had about eight kids. I asked him, but he did not admit to it. He just told me that he knew I would never talk to him if he told me the truth.

"How old are these kids?"

"The oldest is ten."

"So, you're telling me you were thirteen when you got a girl pregnant?"

He laughed a little.

"Were you?"

"Yeah."

"Damn!"

"Shut-up."

"I can't believe you denied your kids. If you denied them, what makes me think you won't deny me?"

We pulled up to his mother's house. He ran in to get something from her. I shook my head, thinking *what have I gotten myself into now? I am about to have a kid by someone that already has four of his own. He has to be lying about his age. He lied about his name, kids, and everything else when he met me. Now, I'm pregnant by this fool. What's next?*

He came back to the car.

"What's wrong?"

"I want to go home."

"Why? We're just going to go to the movies and grab a bite to eat."

"You've lied to me the whole time we've been seeing each other. I should have expected this, but you made me think you were different."

"I didn't lie to you when I told you I loved you."

"You lied about everything else. I'm six months pregnant by someone I don't even know. How do you think I feel about that? One day, you tell me to get an abortion. The next day, you tell me you're glad we're having a child together. Now, you're telling me that you can't help me take care of MY child. I can't continue this."

"I am glad we're having a child together."

"See, you're crazy. You don't know what you want."

We went to the movies. Afterwards, he stopped to get an Oreo shake. I knew that would not go well on my stomach. I didn't order anything. There was a girl walking in the distance. After receiving his shake, he pulled up to her. She was thin and pregnant.

"Hey!"

"Hey!"

"Where are you going? "

"I'm headed to the house. "

"Get in. I'll take you home. "

She got into the car with us.

"Layla, this is my niece, Natasha."

"Hey."

"Hey."

He chatted with her for a while. Then, he dropped her off in front of her house.

"That was my brother's daughter."

"Really."

"Yeah, but he doesn't claim her."

"Wow... Why?"

"He just got caught up with her mom, got her pregnant, and ran off."

I thought, *kind of, like what you're doing.*

"It's sad."

"Yeah."

He didn't take me home. We pulled up to his house.

"JD, I'm not happy right now. I really think I should go home."

"Please. I need you."

"You don't need me."

"You don't understand. I really do love you. I don't want to, but I do. I try to stay away, but I feel like I have to see you."

"You keep making accusations about me that you know aren't true. I have a lot of respect for myself. I'm not completely happy with my decisions, but I wouldn't give myself to just anybody. You know that. I was with you everyday until now. How could I have been with someone else? With you, I feel like I made a huge mistake. Now, I have to pay for it. I have to bring a child into this world by myself because you're not man enough to handle your responsibility. You talked about your brother, but what makes you different?"

I began to cry. I was hurting. I brought this on myself. I should have walked away a long time ago, long before we had taken things this far.

He was sad. He sat with his head down. I knew he wouldn't take me home. We went inside the house. I sat on the loveseat. He bent down to take off my shoes. He stood and held his hand out for me. We walked upstairs to his room, took our clothes off, and lied in the bed. He kissed my forehead and ran his hands through my hair.

"Good night."

"Good night."

I honestly believed that JD wouldn't let me go through this alone. With everything that he was dealing with personally, I still believed he wouldn't do that to me. Why? Because, I knew he cared about me. I could just feel it. He didn't have to say it. I felt that if I just prayed and let God handle my situation, everything would work out. With all of the hell that was in this confusion, only God could handle it. I knew I hadn't made great choices. I was not living my life as I was supposed to. God was my only way out.

I updated JD on everything that was going on with my pregnancy. He spent time with me, but we argued more than anything. I started pushing away from him.

One day, as I was working the ten until six shift, my friend Chase and my brother pulled up to the store. I was so excited to see them.

"What's up?"

"Nothing."

I didn't know if they were smiling because they were glad to see me or because of my stomach. As I was talking to them, JD pulled up with another girl. I continued talking to Chase and Kurt, trying not to let my feelings show. He came and paid for his purchase. He looked me in the eyes. Then, he walked away. As he was walking away, he called into the store.

"Who is that?"

"Chase and my brother. Who is that?"

"A friend."

"A friend?"

"Yeah."

"Okay... I'm going to finish talking to them and I'll call you back."

I talked to Chase and Kurt for a little while longer. When they left, I broke down. My heart was crushed. I could not believe JD had just done that to me. I felt so disrespected. I prayed until I stopped crying.

I didn't return to college. My OB-GYN said that walking the campus in August wasn't a good idea. So, I asked for more hours at the store. I needed to make as much money as possible.

I moved into an apartment. I had a roommate. My rent was almost nothing.

My roommate was cool, but she was afraid of JD. Sometimes, he would sit outside of our apartment or call numerous times, if we didn't answer the phone. I really wanted to be with him, but he was not the same person. The person he had become, I didn't want. He made me very unhappy. In addition, the closer I came to having my child, the more he stopped coming around.

My OB-GYN decided to induce my labor. She stated that she would induce on the fifth of December so that I would have my baby on the sixth.

I went in at midnight. My mom came with me. Hours later, my sister and her friend arrived. I had not heard from JD. I told him, but he didn't show.

I had my daughter on the fifth of December. My doctor told me that I would have her on the sixth. I was okay with the sixth because it was my grandmother's birthday. The fifth was Gregory's.

I stayed with my mom in Atwood for four weeks. It was torture. My car was still in Nashville. I couldn't go anywhere. Some of my friends came by. Still, it wasn't okay. I was so used to having my freedom and leaving whenever I wanted. Now, I didn't have my car and I had a baby.

Some time around Christmas, Gregory found out that I was staying at my mom's house. He stopped by. We sat in the living room and chat. I was a little reluctant when he asked to hold my baby.

"Do you know how to hold a baby?"

"Give me the baby."

"Be careful with her."

I slowly placed her in his hands. He held her to his chest. Tears rolled down his face as he was holding her.

"She was supposed to be mine."

"Don't start this now."

"She was."

"Well, she's not. You're gonna have to get over it."

"What's her name?"

"Dominique."

"That's pretty. A pretty name for a pretty girl. Does she have his last name?"

"No."

"Good. I like her name."

"When did you have her?"

I sighed, "On the fifth."

"That's my birthday!"

"I know."

"You planned that."

"How can I plan to have someone on your birthday? My OB-GYN told me I would have her on the sixth. That's my grand-mother's birthday. She came an hour after my water was broken."

"Whatever."

I shook my head in disbelief. His arrogance hadn't changed a bit. We chat for a while. Then, he headed towards the door.

Gregory and I said our farewells. When he left, I stood at the door, thinking of how many times he had walked out of that same door and I cried, not wanting him to leave. I didn't this time. I felt stronger. I stood, smiling at the thought of the person I was becoming, realizing that God was molding me into the person he wanted me to be. I knew that I still had a long way to go. Nevertheless, I still felt good. I put my hands in the pockets of my jeans and rocked back and forth on my tiptoes.

I didn't call JD. I couldn't believe he didn't come to the hospital. This was my reality check. I honestly believed we were more than that. I didn't cry about it. I prayed. I prayed because, in regards to how much he would help, my child still had to be taken care of. So, when I wasn't strong enough, I knew God would be. I thought, *once again, I must keep going.*

JD's mom agreed to watch Dominique while I worked. This would allow me to make some money while she was able to spend time with her granddaughter. I agreed to pay her ten dollars a day. JD knew nothing about our agreement.

On the first day, JD's mom called.

"Hello!"

"Hey, JD just left."

I was a little startled.

"Can you believe he asked me whose baby I was keeping? I said,

"JD, this is your baby. She looks just like you.""
She continued talking. I didn't think I could take more. I swallowed hard.
"Then, what did he say?"
"He said, "Momma, you know we went through this with another girl. Then, we found out it wasn't my kid." Then I told him that I knew this child was his. He picked her up and held her."
"Why did he pick her up?"
"I don't know. He just picked her up. She's a good baby. She doesn't ever cry."
"I know. I'll be there when I get off."
"Okay."
"Bye."

I hung up. JD's denial really hurt. I felt that all of the love he told me he had for me was a lie.

He pulled up to the store. He motioned for me to let him in. I didn't want him to know I had spoken with his mom. Therefore, I let him in.
"Why is my mom watching the baby? How does she even know about her?"
"Does it matter? She not yours anyway, right?"
I was pissed. Tears began to roll down my face.
"You should leave."
"I didn't want her to know. You don't understand. I have some situations I have to handle."
"Situations that make you deny your own child, JD? If you ever really feel that she's not your child, take the fucking test."
"I know she's mine."
"Why would you say she's not?"
"You don't understand."
"I think you should leave."
He was silent. He had no response. Therefore, he left.
JD's denial hurt so much my stomach was in knots. It hurt so badly, I couldn't cry. I gasped for breath, while holding my stomach. I loved him. I asked God, "How can I love a man that

66

denies his own child?"

At the end of each week, I was supposed to pay his mother. JD agreed to help pay her. The problem was that I was always waiting for him to pay me. Sometimes, it took weeks for him to pay me.

One week, I had used my check on diapers, the hospital bill, rent, and the electric bill. I told her I would pay her as soon as he gave me the money. It had taken him three days to pay me. His mother became angry with me, stating that she needed the money. I took the money from my savings account to pay her.

I was never late paying her after that. She was really upset with me that day.

She had asked me to start bringing the car seat into the house, just in case she needed to leave. I would bring Dominique into the house, while she was asleep in the car seat. Sometimes, I would come to get her and she would still be in the car seat in the same spot that I had put her in before I left. Her diaper would be soaked. This angered me. It went on for weeks. I told my manager about the situation, as I was frustrated. Days later, I received a phone call.
"Hello."
"Hi. My name is Carol Ann. I'm your manager's sister. She told me about your situation. I just wanted you to know that if you need a sitter, I'll do what I can to help. We work different shifts. So, I'll get her when you need me to."
I closed my eyes, thanking God. A few days before the phone call, JD's mother told me that she needed more money for watching Dominique. I couldn't believe her.
I met Carol Ann at her house. She was very nice. She started keeping my child immediately.

One day, after going to his mom's house, JD discovered that his mom was no longer keeping Dominique. He came to the store to ask what happened.
"Where is Dominique? Why is my mom not watching her? "

67

"I found another sitter. I was having problems with your mom. Moreover, she didn't have her priorities together. She told me that she needed me to buy her some bread. So, I bought some. Then, she asked me to buy her something to eat. However, she had money to go and buy cigarettes. That's crazy."

"I told you how she is."

"Yeah, but it's one thing to not have food. It's another to use the money; you do have, on cigarettes."

"How's the new lady?"

"She's really cool. She doesn't smoke. Now, I don't have to worry about my kid coming home smelling like cigarettes."

We chat a while longer. Then, he left.

I decided to return to college when my child was six months old. A friend of our family introduced me to her sitter, Melba. During the day, Melba would baby-sit. At night, Carol Ann would get her.

I completed two classes during summer school. Programming became boring and time consuming. That's when I decided to change my major to Accounting.

For the fall, I took six classes, not realizing how much of a change having a child would be. It was really hard. Sometimes, Carol Ann would get Dominique from Melba because I would be in the library, working and researching.

School was overwhelming. My grades dropped, but I was determined to finish.

Drama

On numerous occasions, one of the guys from my study group came to my job to work on our group assignment. One day, he asked if he could take me to get Dominique. I agreed. On my way to the vehicle, JD pulled up.

"Where are you going?"

"To get Dominique."

"Who is that?"

"One of the guys from my study group. We're actually distant relatives. There's nothing to worry about. I don't date relatives." It was true, but he didn't believe me.

"If you leave with him, I'm going to flatten your tires."

"JD, that's insane!"

I didn't believe him. I continued walking to the vehicle. JD walked over to my car and began to take the air out of my tires. I walked over to JD.

"What are you doing?"

"Tell him to leave."

"You are embarrassing me."

"Tell him to leave."

"Why? We're not together JD. I don't say anything to you when you ride through here with your little friends in the car."

JD became angry. He grabbed my neck and began choking me.

"Stop! Stop!"

He was hysterical. Corry rolled down the window.

"Are you okay?"

JD let go, got in his truck, and left. Coughing, I said, "Yeah." I got in the truck with Corry.

"That guy is crazy."

"I know."

"Did you tell him we were related?"

"Yeah. He didn't believe me. I don't want to talk about him." We started discussing the completion of our project. After getting Dominique, we returned to the store.

"Do you want to stay at my place tonight? I don't think it's safe for you to go home."

"I'll be fine."

As we returned to my car, I noticed that my tires were flat.

"I can't believe him!"

"Are you sure you want to stay at home?"

"Yes, he's crazy, but he wouldn't kill me."

"I don't know. He was choking you earlier."

"I'll be fine."

I put the air back in my tires and drove home. JD called.

"Hello."

"Open the door."

"He's not here, JD."

"Open the door."

I opened the door, JD walked in.

"JD, what's wrong with you? I don't give you any of the problems you give me. You totally embarrassed me tonight. You ride by my job with different girls in the car constantly. I say nothing. If you even see me talking to a guy, you start acting foolish. I don't get it. "

"Every time I turn around, I get a call from one of my boys, telling me that another guy is at your window."

"It's a gas station; they're going to come up there. I can't stop them from getting gas."

"Yeah, but why you got to talk to them?"

"It's a gas station! There's not a guy up there that I want. The guys that I let in the building are in my group. I didn't choose my study group, my teacher did. One of the guys in my group is dating my roommate. Another one, I know from visiting his family in my hometown. The one that was there tonight just found out we were related. My roommate's friend comes there all of the time to chat, but that's it. Maybe you should tell your friends to stop calling you, making assumptions about me."

JD grabbed me, pulling me to him. I lifted my hand to stop him.

"Not tonight. I'm really upset about what you did. You didn't have to choke me."

"I'm sorry."

I sat on my couch, rubbing my hands over my face. I was so confused. I wanted things to be the way they were when we met, but they weren't. His eyes still danced when he was with me, but we were always arguing about something. I didn't know how to fix our relationship.

JD and I continued sleeping together, but it was never the same. It seemed that our sex was always brought on by an argument. I couldn't understand him. He would drive by my job with other girls during the day, but always end up at my place at night. It hurt. I tried to act as if I never saw him with them, but how could I not? I was on an emotional rollercoaster. I knew I had to get myself together. I just didn't know how.

I went to my Black Arts and Literature class one day. Our teacher's assignment was to read the book of Proverbs, choose four verses out of that book, and tell why they were so significant to us. I had never read the whole book of Proverbs. To be honest, I don't remember turning to that book. While at work, when we weren't busy, I read. I had wondered why, of all the books in the Bible, she had chosen Proverbs. She seemed so enthused by it. As I was reading, I found out. I couldn't stop reading. When I reached the twenty-fourth chapter, I circled the first verse, "Be not thou envious against evil men, neither desire to be with them." That verse, alone, was something I could live by. I needed that verse. I thought of JD, how he had lied about everything. I told him I never wanted any dealings with another guy that sold drugs, only to find that he, himself, was selling them. I thought of how he would ride by with other girls, but told me he loved me. I thought of how we would have sex after arguing. That one verse meant so much to me. I cried, right there at the store. I didn't care who watched me.

I decided to never sleep with JD again. If that were the only thing that I was doing wrong, I would fix it. At first, it was hard. JD started accusing me of sleeping with other men because I wasn't sleeping with him. He also began to say that I had my child to trap him. Everything he said began to sound insane.

I began going to church every Sunday and Wednesday. I had to keep myself on the right path. I knew that not going would cause me to get off that path. Therefore, I went whenever I could. I needed to rid myself of demons.

I began to watch my language. I realized it was unlady-like to use profanity. I thought of how people would perceive me if I continued talking that way. In addition, I thought about my child. Children mimic what they hear.

Not using profanity was the easier of the two. Although it was hard to admit, I loved sex. I was having it three or more times a day with JD. Therefore, it was really hard to just stop. I felt like an addict trying to get off drugs. I tried to see him as less as possible. I also told him about what I had read and how I felt about it. He wasn't too thrilled with my comments.

Making changes in my life caused JD to assume that I was seeing someone else. He began to drive by my place often. If I weren't there, he would call to see where I was. He began to annoy me. Sometimes, I wouldn't answer the phone.

One day, I was at the laundry mat washing clothes when JD called. My phone was in my car. As my clothes were drying, I walked outside to get my phone. JD had called over ten times. I returned his call. He was hysterical.
"Where are you?"
"I'm washing clothes at the laundry mat."
"Who's with you?"
"What do you mean?"
"Who's with you?"
"Dominique."
"I'm coming up there."
"Why? I'm just washing clothes."
"Which one."
"The one that's down the street from the apartment."
I became frustrated with him.

72

"JD, you should really just leave us alone. You don't trust me. You don't pay me. If you do, it's never on time. You don't take care of your responsibility. You deny us. So, just let us be."
"Are you seeing somebody else?"
"No, I already told you that! Just stop calling me."
"I will kill you!"
"What kind of comment is that?"
I hung up, not wanting to entertain that conversation.
 I folded my clothes and headed home. Something told me not to go, but I was heading there. As I was about to pull up to the house, I noticed JD's car parked in front of a truck. I sped away, thinking about what he had said. He began chasing me. I pulled into an alley, but he cut in front of me, stopping me from going forward. I put my car in reverse. He jumped out of his car with something in his hand. I called the police as I had put my car in reverse. JD jumped on my car. I stopped because I didn't want to hurt him. I covered my face with my hands as I was telling the operator my location, thinking that's where they would find me. JD got off my car and held up his cell phone. When I noticed it was his phone, I sped away. I drove around the neighborhood, trying to rationalize what had just happened. I told the police that I was okay. They asked if I wanted to press charges. I told them no. JD began to call my phone as I was walking into the house. I answered.
"JD, what is wrong with you? Threatening to kill me, jumping on my car, are you crazy?"
"You won't talk to me!"
"Do you think that killing me is going to make me talk to you? Does that make sense?"
"No."
"Why didn't you just say you wanted to talk?"
"You weren't answering my calls."
"My phone was in my car."
"Can I come over?"
"I don't know."
"Open the door."

He was outside. I was afraid, but I didn't want him to notice. I unlocked the door. He walked in and pulled me to him.

"I'm sorry."

I didn't push him away. I cried while he held me. I felt like I needed him. I loved JD, but sometimes, talking to him is like trying to wake the dead. I knew he cared about me, but something held him back and he took his frustration out on me. One minute, he wanted to be with me. The next, he couldn't. I didn't understand it. He couldn't explain it. So, our problems continued.

Just when I thought I was ahead financially, I had a car accident. The man that hit me was driving a stolen vehicle. My insurance had cancelled about two months earlier. Carol Ann came to the scene of the accident. She drove us home.

I didn't want to stay home, feeling sorry for myself. Therefore, I went to work. JD rode by my job over and over again, not knowing that I was there. Finally, he stopped.

"I rode by to see if you were here."

I didn't tell him that I saw him.

"What's up?"

"Can you let me in?"

I opened the door.

"Where's your car?"

"I had an accident."

"Why are you at work?"

"I couldn't stay home feeling sorry for myself. So, I just came in."

"How'd you get here?"

"Kevin brought me."

"Why didn't you call me?"

"I figured you were busy. Kevin was in the area. So, I just had him to bring me."

"Are you seeing him now?"

"No, we're just friends. He's not what I want at all."

Anger was building in JD. Many women were after Kevin, but not me. He wasn't for me. Kevin was the man that took advantage of people that needed him. It was an "I look out for you, you give me what I want" kind of deal. Kevin did help me, but I only shared my knowledge of the Bible with him.

I didn't tell JD that. He wouldn't believe me anyway. Therefore, I told him the truth, that I wasn't sleeping with Kevin. He was still upset. So, he left.

Kevin pulled up later that night. We were chatting about life when JD pulled up. He motioned for me to let him in. It was a little confusing to me. I let him in. He spoke to Kevin and asked me to come to the back.

"I thought you weren't seeing him."

"If I was, do you think you would be in here too?"

"Kiss me."

"Why?"

"Do you love me?"

"I do, but JD, you're not ready for what I have to offer. You said it yourself."

"That doesn't mean I don't love you. "

"I know, but the way you're going about things is all wrong. You make me not want to be with you. Riding by with different girls in the car doesn't help. It hurts. If that's your way of trying to make me jealous, it's not working. You're just pushing me farther and farther away. I can't believe you would do something like that to hurt me anyway. You shouldn't want to hurt me."

JD left. I walked to the front of the store to talk to Kevin.

"Why did you let him in?"

"I don't know."

"You in love with him."

I didn't respond.

"Man, he's a nobody. I'm mad at you for that."

"Kevin, I don't care. I just want to keep down the confusion."

"You don't owe him anything. That man rides by with other girls in the car like you mean nothing to him."

"That doesn't mean that I have to do the same."

"Alright, I'm gone."

The next day, JD came by to take me to get the rest of my belongings from my car. He observed the damage as I was getting everything out.

"I think your car can be fixed."

"Maybe, but, I don't want it. It will never be the same."

"I'm glad you two weren't hurt."

"Yeah, me too."

"What if I bought it?"

"Why would you want to buy a wrecked car?"

"I'll get it fixed. Then, I can drive around and think of you."

"Whatever. You can have it."

He walked to the office. I took the title out of the car and signed it over to him.

We talked as we rode back to the house. Somewhere, in the midst of our conversation, JD said, "Let's have another child together."

"There's no way I would have another child with you. You don't take care of the first child we have together."

He laughed, "It will be different."

I didn't entertain it. I just let him talk.

JD had the car fixed. Then, he started driving it. It felt a little awkward seeing him driving around in my old car.

One day, the car passed by the store. I waved, thinking he was driving it, but it wasn't him. There was a woman driving my car. There were kids in the back. I was so angry.

I changed jobs for multiple reasons. I didn't tell JD. He would eventually figure it out. I was just relieved to leave that store. The drama was becoming overwhelming. In addition, he wouldn't be able to ride by with his friends. If I didn't see them, it couldn't bother me.

I could never understand his reason for riding by my job with other girls in the car, but it made my heart ache. It ached because I used to be that girl. At first, we were so cool, I never believed he would stop coming around. I didn't believe any of this would have happened. Facing reality caused so much pain.

JD stopped paying me after I left the store. I didn't mind because I needed to be away from him. I loved him. Not having him in my life was like dealing with a loved one's death. I believed that the less I saw him, the less I would think of him. That wasn't true. I longed for him, for his touch, and for his dancing eyes. Nevertheless, I knew he didn't need to be in my life at that moment.

Carol stopped charging me, stating that she saw what I was going through with working, going to school, and trying to raise my child alone. She was a blessing.

I also had two other sitters named Naomi and Margaret. They, too, stopped charging me.

I moved in with my sister after someone had broken into my apartment while I was on vacation. I had an idea of who had done it, but that person never admitted to it. It was strange that my daughter's money jar was the only thing taken from my apartment.

I thought that moving in with my sister would help me to save money and give me extra time to focus on school. I was wrong. My vehicle was constantly breaking down on me. I spent thousands of dollars trying to fix my vehicle.

I paid my sister twenty-five dollars less than what I was paying in rent. I assumed everything would be fine. It was not. Even though we worked very different shifts, my sister found herself wanting time alone, without me being in the house. She would tell me to find somewhere to stay for the weekend, and sometimes, a whole week. So, I stayed at Kevin's house. We slept in totally different beds.

I began to depend on Kevin because he was always there to help. I had other friends that were there for me, but I always had somewhere to lay my head with no worries when I was over to Kevin's house.

One day, when I was working at Target, one of my sister's friends stepped into my lane to check out.

"Tree?"

"Yeah!"

"Hmmm. Sana said you wouldn't amount to anything. She was right. You over here working at Target. When you gone graduate?"

I didn't respond. Some of the customers were looking at me, waiting for me to say something. I said nothing. I wanted to cry. I wanted to run, but I didn't. I stayed there, ringing up my customers. When I left work, her words played repeatedly in my head. I never said anything to my sister about it. Although I didn't believe that she said that about me, it hurt.

One day, as I was at church, my pastor said, "If you are living with your family and they can put you out whenever they want, you are homeless."

I cried. I felt homeless, having to find somewhere to stay when my sister wanted to be alone. I also spent more money staying there than I was spending when I was living alone. My sister and I were constantly arguing. When my car would break down, I would have to call friends to come and get me. Her excuse was that she wanted me to be responsible. More and more, the feeling of being homeless kicked in. I cried daily. I prayed constantly.

I wasn't making enough money to leave, but I couldn't take it anymore. I prayed that God would just be there to help me through the rough times. I called my landlord and moved back into my old apartment. I was so angry with my sister that I didn't tell her. I just moved. I really don't believe she ever meant to hurt me. I knew things would be better if I lived on my own rather than living with her.

God was there for me. I was never a day late paying my rent. One day, I called my landlord to tell him that I would be late making my payment because I didn't have the money.

"That's fine. It's not due until the first. That's a week from now. Plus, you're the only person here that has never been late paying me."

"I know it's not due, but my paycheck will not be enough to cover my rent."

"Well, that's fine."

"Thank you."

As I hung up, I cried. I got on my knees to pray, but someone knocked on my door.

I went to the door. My friend, Vincent, was standing there. I had wiped my tears away as I was walking to the door.

"Hey, little sis, what's going on?"

"Nothing. Just getting ready for bed."

"Can you talk for a minute?"

"Yeah."

Vincent was venting about his kids' mother and how she wouldn't let him spend time with them. His fists were balled and tears rolled from his eyes as he expressed how much he loved his children. He told me that he knew God would take care of things. We chat a while longer. Then, he left.

I never told Vincent what I was going through. I didn't want to throw my problems out there when he was dealing with his own. As I was getting ready to lie down, the phone rang.

"Hello."

"Hey, little sis."

"Hey, what's up?"

"I really appreciated being able to talk to you about my problems."

"No problem."

"I knew that if I handed it to you, you wouldn't take it. But, I played the lotto yesterday and won twenty thousand dollars. I knew you would reject the money. So, when you walked to the kitchen to get something to drink, I hid it under the pillow on the couch. Love you, little sis."

Vincent hung up. I walked over to the pillow and lifted

it. Almost three months of my rent was under that pillow. I paid for two months the next day. I deposited the rest.

Only God knew what I was going through. That's when I realized how true the statement "never more than we can bear" was. I thanked God.

The First Call

I was checking my messages one day after work, when an unfamiliar voice on the other end said, "My name is Michelle. I'm JD's kids' mom. I was calling all of his whores to let them know that I have his phone while he is incarcerated." Then, she just hung up the phone. I started to call back, but I decided against it. She seemed hateful. (Also, because she had just called me a whore.) I remembered the stories I had heard of her, thinking about how it encouraged me to never want to talk to her. It would be almost a year later that I would hear that voice again.

I had started seeing a guy named Jamar. I liked Jamar's admiration for me. He acknowledged my strengths and abilities. We always talked about our goals and how we would achieve them. Because of that, he would always say, "How was JD ever able to walk into your life?" After finding out who JD really was, I wondered the same. In regards to what I found out about JD, it was still hard for me to believe that the person that I had known was the same person that I found out he was. Even then, I thought of all of the good times we had, longing for those moments.

Often, people would come to me and say bad things about JD, but I couldn't stop loving him. I tried so hard to keep him off my mind.

Jamar couldn't fulfill those times. I knew that. He was all work and no play, always trying to conjure up a way to obtain a little cash.

Once, we had gone to the park. We were playing catch with my football. For a while, everything was okay. Then, he continuously threw the ball to the side of me, so that I would have to run to catch it. I stopped running. He said, "You've gotta work for it!" I thought, *this is not fun. It's work.*

My relationship with Jamar did not last long. It ended abruptly with his ex-girlfriend's involvement. He continuously told me that she was moving out because he didn't want to be with her anymore. He also stated that she was buying a larger house, but managed her money poorly and never saved.

I believed him. He seemed to be completely honest with me. We had been seeing each other for a month with no problems. One day, he asked to stay at my place to get away from her, stating that he wanted her to get her things and leave. Jamar seemed so unhappy. Therefore, I let him stay. He slept in the living room on a mattress.

Another night, he called. He sounded as if he was in a hurry.

"Hey."

"Hey."

I'm getting ready to jump in the shower and I'll be on my way over."

"Okay."

"Alright."

I had noticed the rush in his voice before he hung up. My phone began to ring again. It was his number, so I picked up.

"Hey."

"Who is this…Who in the fuck is this?"

I hung up, startled by the woman screaming on the other end. She called back. She was crying.

"Hello."

"I'm sorry for screaming at you."

I said nothing. I did not know what to say. My stomach was in knots. She continued talking.

"I knew something was going on. Jamar hasn't been coming home. He doesn't answer my calls. He always seems excited when he leaves. Every Wednesday, he's been grabbing his Bible and going to Bible Study."

"He meets me at church on Wednesdays. He told me that you were moving out and that it was over between the two of you."

"He didn't lie. I am moving out…but he is supposed to come

with me."

"So, you two are together."

"No, but, I want us to be."

"If you want to be with him, it's fine. I'll step aside."

"Will you?"

"Yes."

"What's your name?"

"Layla."

"Layla, I love him so much. I know he doesn't feel the same way. It's been hurting me to see him walk out of here so happy. By the way, my name is Karen."

"Karen, I apologize for this whole misunderstanding…."

"Okay. He just got out of the shower. I have to go."

She hung up. I sat in the dark. I didn't know what to think of the conversation I had just had. I wanted to just call and say, "Stay home. You belong with her." I tried to imagine how Karen felt. Her love for him was sincere. She was truly hurting.

As I was sitting on my couch, the phone began to ring again. It was Jamar. They were arguing.

"Four years, Jamar! We've been together for four years! You're going to let some girl come in the middle of that."

Jamar was very nonchalant.

"Hello….hello!"

"Hey."

"I'm on my way."

"No. Jamar, you can't come here."

"Why?"

"Because you're hurting her."

He began to yell at her, telling her that she was ruining everything. I hung up. I didn't want any drama.

A week later, I received a phone call from a number that I hadn't seen before.

"Hello."

"Layla?"

It was Karen.

"Layla, this is Karen."

"Hi."

"Hey. Things have been really hard this past week. I realize that Jamar is not happy here. So, I was calling to tell you that I'm okay with you two seeing each other. It's hard because I love him. But, knowing how he feels, knowing that I'm not making him happy, makes it easier to let go. It seems that he really cares for you."

I was speechless. I managed to say, "Are you sure this is what you want? Can you really let go?"

"…..Yes."

We hung up after finishing our discussion. Karen sounded so heartbroken. I was a little confused. I sat down on the couch, trying to relate to her feelings. The phone rung again. This time it was Jamar.

"Layla, I've been longing to see you again. I miss you so much. Can I come and see you?"

"Jamar, I really didn't like your attitude with Karen. Maybe you should have tried to put yourself in her shoes before you made your decision."

"I know. I know…Can I see you?"

I contemplated on seeing Jamar. I knew that he liked me. There was something about him that I liked also. I think it's the fact that he was a go-getter, motivator, and a thinker. I thought that he was what I needed.

There was also something that I didn't like. I just couldn't put my hands on it.

"Yeah, you can come."

"I'm on my way."

About twenty minutes later, I heard a knock at the door. I let Jamar in.

"Did you cook today?"

"Actually, I did."

He sat down to eat.

"You know, this is really good."

"Thanks."

84

I realized that I wasn't really attracted to Jamar. I liked his attraction to me. The more I looked at him, the more I pondered on whether or not I could be with him. I figured, time will tell.

It was getting late. My daughter had fallen asleep. Jamar and I were sitting in my living room.

"Can I stay?"

"No, you should leave."

"Layla, I want to sleep with you so bad."

I could tell he did by the way he looked at me. Plus, he was always feeling on my thighs and hips. I didn't know whether to be turned on or off by it.

That night, I was also turned on. I longed for a male companion. I didn't want my flesh to get the best of me. So, I sent him home.

Never stopping Jamar from coming over late was my mistake. Letting him stay was even worse. One day, I gave in to him. Then, he started carrying on about how we should have a child together. To me, it was an insane statement, but he was serious.

Karen began to call again to see if Jamar was with me.

"Hello!"

"Hey."

"Hey, Karen."

"Hey, Is Jamar over there?"

"Yeah, he's here."

"Can I talk to him for just a second?"

"Yeah, hold on."

I handed the phone to Jamar. They began to argue. He hung up, but she called back. I handed the phone to him. He didn't answer.

"Why don't you answer the phone?"

"Because, she's not talking about anything."

"You have to talk to her. I don't want any problems with her."
"She's crazy."
The phone began to ring again.
"Don't answer that."
I answered because I didn't want her to get mad at me.
"Layla, I still love Jamar. I know he wants to be with you, but I'm not going to make this easy for you."
"What do you mean?"
"It's not fair for him to just walk out of my life like I was nothing."
"That has nothing to do with me."
"Yeah but, you're the problem. If I can get you out of the way. He'll see that we belong together."
"I thought you said that everything was fine."
"I thought it was, but it wasn't. You're in the way."
"Karen, this is insane. One minute you're okay, the next you're not. It doesn't make sense."
Jamar grabbed the phone and hung up. Karen called back. He held the phone, knowing that I would answer. She called a few more times, but he had silenced the phone. I became annoyed with the whole situation.
"Jamar, maybe you should go back to her. I don't want any problems. I'm not afraid of her, but she sounds crazy. She's back and forth about her acceptance. She keeps calling. I don't want any drama."
"She'll eventually stop."
"I want her to stop now."
"Let's just lie down and go to sleep."
As we lay down to sleep, I noticed the light on my phone going off and on. Karen was calling.

The next day, I checked my phone. Her last call was at 3:40 a.m. She had also left messages. They were not nice.

Almost everyday after that, she called. I became angry with both of them, her for calling, him because she was calling.

One day, the circus was in town. He had asked me to come

with him. I went. That night, when we came in from the circus, she called. She left a message, telling me that she was there with him the previous day.

"Did you take her to the circus yesterday?"

"Yes, but because she's close to my family."

"You should leave."

"Why?"

"Because I'm not okay with that."

"I only did it...."

"Just leave."

"You don't understand."

"Leave."

Jamar left. He began to call. I didn't answer. I slept.

Jamar called multiple times for the next two weeks afterwards, leaving apologetic messages. I never responded. I wanted to rid myself of him.

A few weeks later, Karen called.

"He's not here."

"I know. You must have kicked his ass to the curb. Girl, he's been calling, trying to make up, and everything. I knew you had let him go."

"Yeah, he's all yours."

She laughed.

"Hey, I'm sorry I gave you such a hard time," she said.

"It's okay. It's over now."

We settled our differences, said our farewells, and hung up. I was so relieved.

For the past few weeks since making Jamar leave, I had been vomiting all over the place. If I passed someone with a bad odor, I would vomit. It was constant. It was making work complicating. I went to the doctor only to find that I was pregnant. I couldn't believe it. I wanted nothing to do with Jamar. I wanted him and Karen out of my life completely. I contemplated. I was against abortions, but I didn't want to bring another child into this world alone. So, I called Jamar.

"Hello."

"We have to talk."

"I miss you."

I didn't entertain that conversation. I wanted to discuss our situation.

We agreed to meet. I decided that I would be as forward with him as possible. I didn't want him to think there was any way we could possibly get back together.

"Jamar, I'm pregnant."

"Really!"

He seemed excited.

"Yes, but, I'm not having it."

"Why? Don't I get some input in this?"

"Jamar, I have had enough drama from you and Karen. I don't want another child by someone I don't plan on being with."

"What do you want me to do?"

"Help pay for the abortion."

"Why, when I don't want you to have it?"

I began to cry.

"I don't want to be with you, Jamar. I don't want anything with you."

He walked away.

He called a few days later.

"Hello."

"Can we talk?"

"What?"

"I really think that you should consider having this child. I'll help you as much as I can."

"You don't get it. I don't want any connections with you."

"Was I that bad?"

"Jamar…I've already scheduled my appointment. I just need you to pick me up. They told me that the drugs wouldn't allow me to drive."

"How much do I owe you?"

We paid cash for the abortion. I was extremely nervous. I felt horrible about the abortion, but I knew that I needed him out of my life. I did not want any connections to him. I was sure of it.

There were a lot of women in the room with me, waiting on the same procedure. Everyone was talking, telling how many times they had already been there. I was silently listening, disgusted with some of their statements. One girl already had five kids at home. This was her third procedure. One girl looked over at me, but my pill had already kicked in.

"You look out of it."

"I am."

"Is this your first time?"

"Yes."

"You look high."

"The medicine has kicked in."

"You only had one pill. You must not do any drugs."

"I don't."

"No wonder. You ever taken ecstasy?"

"No."

"Any pills?"

"No."

Another girl across the room said, "Girl, leave her alone."

"I needed two pills for mine to kick in. She only had one and she's in the zone."

They were laughing. I was next in line for the procedure.

As my procedure began, I thought of how I had downed other women for the procedure. I couldn't believe I was becoming one of them. I became angry with myself for getting so out of hand and making so many stupid decisions. I asked myself what more does it take for me to get on the right path.

When the procedure was finished, I sat. I was very uncomfortable from the sanitary napkin I was wearing, but also, from the procedure itself.

Jamar picked me up. I was still out of it from the pill. He helped me to the car. We sat in silence. All that I could think of was what I had just done.

We pulled into the apartment complex. I stayed on the second floor. He helped me to the building. He came in. We chat for a moment. Then, he started talking about the possibilities of us being together. My medicine was really working on me.

"Hey, I'll talk to you later."

"Who's going to pick up Dominique?"

"I will as soon as this medicine wears off."

"When will that happen?"

"I don't know, but I have hours before I have to get her."

"Do you want me to stay here?"

"No, I'll be fine. You go back to work."

I could hardly keep my eyes open.

"Are you sure you want me to leave?"

"I'm positive."

He left. I cried myself to sleep. The abortion was all that I could think about. I envisioned the child standing with its hands open asking me, "Why?" That vision exists for over a year.

Ridding Myself of Drama

I stayed in Church as much as possible. I wanted to rid myself of drama, make the best choices for myself and my child, and fulfill God's purpose on my life. Finding God, I decided, was my only way to clear my head of problems. It was also my way of finding myself. I figured that once I identified myself, I could identify my problems, realizing that I was the source of my problems.

The more I grew in the word, the more I learned of all of my possibilities. I began to read books of the Bible, trying to see God's position throughout the circumstances that had risen, reading about all of the miracles that Jesus had performed. The more I learned, the more I read. I was amazed with everything that they had done. I even spoke with coworkers about some of the miracles that I had read about. Some of my coworkers stated that they didn't believe everything in the Bible, but that they did believe in God. Hearing that helped me to realize why so many people believed major accomplishments were impossible.

One day, JD came by my job, stating that he needed to talk. He told me that, months ago, Michelle had found his password to his phone and had checked his messages. I was on some of the messages she had checked. Supposedly, she was going to ask me a few questions about receiving money from him. He explained that Michelle was very manipulative. He told me to deny everything. I stated that I would handle it.

The call came sooner than I thought. I was working when she called.
"Hello."
"Hi, this is JD's kid's mother. My name is Michelle."
"Okay."
"How do you know JD?"
"We were friends. I met him when I was in school."

"At TSU?"

"Yes. That was a long time ago."

"Is he paying you?"

"No."

"Okay. That's all that I wanted to know."

"Okay."

We hung up. I walked away from my desk to retrieve some papers. When I came back, my phone had a missed call on it. It was Michelle again. She left a message stating that, a while back, she had checked JD's messages. I was on the message saying, "Today is Friday." She also told me that her daughter told her that a woman in a Camry had pulled up to his house with a little girl. He was standing by the car talking. When she walked to the car, the woman left. The little girl said something as they were pulling off, but he covered her ears so that she couldn't hear. She said, "So, after putting two and two together, I just wanted to know if you have a child by him."

I debated on telling her. I didn't have any drama. So, I didn't want any drama. Friday was the day we agreed that he would pay me. He was always late, if he paid. Therefore, I always had to call to remind him.

The other incident was true also. We stopped by his house to get the money one day. His daughter was standing outside. JD came to the car to pay me. His daughter headed to the car minutes later. I pulled off.

"Who is that girl?" my daughter asked.

"That's your sister."

Unexpectedly she yelled, "Sister, sister!"

"Dominique, stop!"

I let the window up as JD covered the girl's ears.

"Why can't I talk to her?"

"She doesn't know you. I do not think it would be a good idea. We do not need any drama. We've had enough."

"Why would we have problems with them?"

"I just heard that their mother isn't nice. From her previous phone call, I can agree. I have had enough problems from your

92

dad alone. We're doing just fine now."

"Okay."

She sat in the back seat with her head down.

I called one of my friends to chat with him about the whole situation after Michelle had called.

"Hello."

"Hey. What's up?"

"Nothing."

"Remember when I told you that Dominique's dad came by to tell me that his other kid's mom would be calling me?"

"Yeah."

"She called today."

"What did she say?"

"She wanted to know if I had a kid by him."

"Did you tell her?"

"No."

"Why?"

"I don't want any problems. I thought that if I told her no, I would be helping him deny my child. If I say yes, I'll probably have to deal with some unnecessary drama."

"Why do you say that? Isn't she older?"

"Yes. She's his age, but what does that mean?"

"I would think she was mature enough to accept your child. She's not married to him. Is she?"

"No."

"So, tell her."

"I don't know. A few people have warned me about her. I would think that she wasn't that way because she's older, but what does that mean? There's a lot of older people that act like kids."

"You shouldn't help him. He's already had it easy."

"It's not for his benefit. It's for my peace of mind."

"However you want to see it."

I gave a lot of thought to the whole situation. I had been debating on whether or not to tell her since JD came to me about it. I returned Michelle's call.

"Hello."

"Hello, Michelle this is Layla."

I told her the truth. She seemed upset. She asked questions. I answered. Then, she asked if we could meet so that her kids could meet my daughter. I agreed. She stated that she didn't live far. So, I told her that we could meet on Charlotte.

It seemed that the more we talked, the angrier she was becoming. I was beginning to second-guess meeting her. I explained that we didn't want any problems and that my child was innocent. Seemingly, she understood.

JD called ten minutes later.

"Why did you tell her?"

"Because I'm not going to help you lie about my child."

"You don't know what you just did."

"What do you mean?"

"You don't know her."

He sounded panicky. He was scaring me.

"What's the problem, JD?"

"She's not the person she made you think she is. You don't know her."

After the conversation with him, I was sure I wasn't ready to meet her. I didn't want her to harm us. So, I called to tell her that I wasn't ready to meet them.

"Hello."

"Michelle, I don't think this is a good time to meet."

"You better be there."

"Now, I know I'm not."

She became demanding. I hung up the phone. She started calling and leaving messages.

JD called later, warning me about Michelle, telling me that I should have never told her. I agreed.

On my way to get Dominique, Michelle called. She and JD were together. They were arguing. I told her that I had to go. I really didn't want to hear them arguing.

I never thought that the situation would get so out

of hand. I was working as the Operations Assistant at a bank. Michelle began to call my job, making threats. My HR director and boss came to me. They stated that she called them and threatened to come on my job. I was told to file a police report against her. I apologized to everyone for the problems.

I talked to the police officer. He asked many personal questions. He seemed so disgusted with me. For a minute, I was ashamed, but JD was my past. The police officer told me to discontinue any communication with JD and don't answer any phone calls from Michelle.

Michelle continued to call. She would leave messages. I never called back. Then, she started blocking her number. When, I answered, she would hang up. Sometimes, I thought JD called and did the same out of anger.

One day, I became so depressed about the whole situation. I was tired of her calling and hanging up. My friend, Bryant, came over. I told him everything.

"I told her, but I never expected for things to be like this. I thought she would understand."

"Don't worry about it."

"I'm not worried about her harming me. She's trying to make me lose my job."

"Let's just pray about it."

I was surprised to hear him say that. I had never prayed with someone over an issue. He prayed first. Then, I prayed. As I prayed, I cried, thinking about the choices that I had made in the past and how they were affecting me at the time. When we finished praying, I felt instant relief. It's as if God reassured me that what I was praying for was already taken care of. I drifted into a deep sleep feeling God's presence, knowing that he was covering me.

The calls continued for a while, but my worrying no longer existed. I had received confirmation in God's revelation at church one Wednesday. The Bishop talked about five things for peace of mind. The fifth thing was, "Worry Over Nothing, Pray Over Everything". I needed that.

After a while, the calls stopped. I was relieved, but disappointed. I hoped that Michelle would take the time out to think on her actions and how they were affecting our children. I prayed for her.

I knew that I needed to make more changes in my life, but I couldn't see what the changes were. I stayed in church, looking for guidance. I began to ask friends to come with me. None came. They began to stop coming around, telling me that I wasn't the same. At first, I asked God why I was losing my friends. I went to church and the Bishop said, "Some people can't handle your change. When they come around you, they talk about the old you, but that's not you anymore. So, they run."

Others did come. I was able to hear so many testimonies from other men and women. I was amazed. Still, some of them also walked away season after season. I went to church and the Bishop talked about the length of time a person may stay in your life.

I began to see my environment changing. Along with that change, my ways of thinking began to change.

In my teenage years, we had so many people to come in and out of our home. Anything from money to underwear would be missing at times. When I moved out of my mother's house, I became stingy. I believed that everything I had was mine. When I had my child, I realized that wasn't true. I had to share when I didn't want to. From my child, I learned that giving not only made me feel good, but the receiver also. On numerous occasions, my child would bring things home from school to share with me. Then, I found that she was doing the same at school. I thanked God for not letting my ways affect her.

The more I stayed in church, the more confirmation I received. I looked back over my life and realized that many things didn't have to happen. I made many bad choices. So, I prayed that God wouldn't let anyone else have to live that life. From attending church services, I learned to have respect for, to love, and to make better choices for myself. It was not a discussion in my home when I was growing up.

I learned about generational curses. How they affected me, how to relieve myself of them, and how to discontinue them in the generations to come. I realized that I had to; first, see them in order to change them.

I learned about the warnings God gives us before we make bad decisions. That sermon, alone, was significant to me. Every situation that I got myself into came with warnings. I ignored my warnings.

The closer I got to God, the more relieved I felt. I realized that for every problem, Jesus is the answer. I wanted others to know and realize that we have choices. We don't have to live a horrible life. He doesn't bring us here for us to be unhappy. Things do happen, but for a reason. We have to learn to appreciate life and God's presence in it.

At some point in time, I realized that what I know now could make a difference in the lives of others. It was an absolute revelation from God. But, for a year, pride caused my flesh to run. I was more worried about how people would look at me after revealing myself than I was about making changes. I asked God if I really had to share everything. It was then that I realized the more things I held back, the more those things would continue. So, I started talking to people about God. The more I read about him, the more I shared. I wanted to get the word out.

One of the most important things that came out of all of this is realizing that in every situation I was in, when no one else was there to help; God was there, covering me, keeping me sane and safe. Seeing this made me love him. I love him because I know there is no one that will ever come into my life that will do the things for me that he has done. Because I know this, I love him more. I love him because he loves me. My prayers have become conversations. I know that what I say to God will go no further.

I still have more growing to do. Although they're not the same as before, I still make mistakes and ignore some of my warnings. I realize that growing is something we have to do constantly. Therefore, staying in the word of God, and surrounding ourselves with others that believe what we believe is very important.

We have to stay away from pessimists that tell us that our dreams are impossible, especially when God says nothing is impossible. Getting to know God and what he can do for us is very important.

Acknowledgements

First, I want to thank God. I want to thank him for everything, for helping me to swallow my pride and withstand humility in order to become a blessing to others. I want to thank him for this vision and helping me to overcome all of the events that took place in the process of bringing this vision into existence. Thank you!!!

I want to thank my family. I want to thank my mother for doing what she had to do to raise the four of us. When I was young, I didn't understand what it was like to be a single mother. I didn't understand the ups and downs, time management, or anything associated with taking care of a child alone. Now, I know that it's hard. So, I thank you.

I want to thank all of my siblings. I want to thank all of you for putting up with me. Thank you for supporting me through everything, even your help with my child.

I want to thank my child also. I don't think I would have ever changed if God didn't bring you into my life. I had to change because I wanted to be a positive example in your life.

I want to thank all of my friends, supporters, and everyone that will purchase this book. I pray that this book helps everyone to make better choices and to love and respect yourselves. Be blessed!

La Wanda